AF231682

HOMO SAPIENS 2.0
Introduction to a Natural History of Hyperinformation

Gérard Ayache

HOMO SAPIENS 2.0
Introduction to a Natural History of Hyperinformation

Max Milo Éditions, Paris, 2023
www.maxmilo.com
ISBN : 978-2-31501-154-4

"I have given you no fixed place, no face of your own, no special gifts, O Adam, so that you may desire, conquer and possess your place, your face and your gifts for yourself. Nature also encloses other species in laws established by Me. But you, whom no boundary limits, by your own will, into whose hands I have placed you, you define yourself. [...] I have made you neither celestial, nor terrestrial, nor mortal, nor immortal, so that, sovereign of yourself, you may freely complete your own form, like a painter or sculptor. You may degenerate into inferior forms, like those of beasts, or, regenerated, attain the superior forms that are divine."

John Pico della Mirandola
De dignitate hominis, 1486.

Prologue

To write a book entitled *Histoire naturelle de l'hyperinformation (Natural history of hyperinformation)* seems presumptuous, for it is a natural history of life. Information is part of life, like matter or energy to physicists; it is its intrinsic substance. The history of life, and then the history of mankind, is basically a history of information.

The first living organism born in the protoplasmic soup nearly 4 billion years ago already knew how to inform itself and others. Much later, *Homo sapiens didn't* become *sapiens* until he could speak, i.e. organize reproducible sounds endowed with meaning. He was then given the tragic opportunity to think, dream and project. By constantly inventing ways to expand, he conquered not only every territory on earth, but also the secrets of matter, energy and life. *Homo sapiens* had slowly grown, he had built what no other animal on earth had done. He had produced so many works, so much art, so much thought. He had launched so many projects, realized so many crazy dreams, invented so many amazing machines. He had even taken himself for God, or at least his proxy on earth. True, he had also let his instincts run wild at times, and committed a few atrocities, but that's the way man is... His path is littered with spectres and monuments, for man has made a Faustian pact: all his works have two flip sides, good and evil. They are capable of both the best and the worst. He was painfully aware of this when he opened the Pandora's box of matter and set it free. This should have been a warning. But it wasn't. Man continued on his forced march, unaware that he was gradually becoming the plaything of the instruments of domination he himself had created.

His great conquest was the mastery of information. It was his obsession from an early age. How could he preserve the traces of his memory and his brief time on this earth? He constantly invented new techniques to communicate further and further away, pushing back the frontiers of space. Proud of the scope of his discoveries, the man was unaware of their nature. Indeed, each of his works not only eluded him, but took on a life of its own. Each of his projections, each of these techniques whose prodigies were praised, took on, unwittingly, a quasi-metaphysical nature. Each of them codified the world in its own way, unifying it, developing certain senses to the detriment of others, favoring certain emotional or intellectual inclinations while neglecting others. Each of his works, from the most moving to the most trivial, possessed a power of an ecological nature. Every one of his inventions changed the world, even though he sincerely believed that it was only adding something to it, a simple step forward in progress. But a drop of wine in a glass of water radically changes the nature of water. The printed book changed the world and transformed man, just as radio, television and the multimedia computer later did. He wasn't aware of it. He couldn't have been, because his works possess a particular force, that of myth. As soon as they are born, his creations melt into the natural order of things. The alphabet, the wheel, light, the car, the plane, the computer, newspapers, TV - all the products of human culture become like gifts from nature, like trees or stars.

But within the space of a century, *Homo sapiens* learned to unlock the secrets of information and its alchemy, and unleashed hyperinformation. This force then undertook subtle alliances between matter and thought, the animate and the inanimate, the virtual and the real. From then on, everything changed. That day, he realized that the power of his brain was eluding him. He realized that he had changed, and so had his world. The niche he had built for himself, century after century, in the long course of his history, had suddenly become alien to him, potentially hostile and dangerous. He discovered, suddenly sober, that his actions, his thoughts, his culture, his habits, his customs, his progress, had de-naturalized his world. And that, what's more, he himself had also changed. He was not quite the same. Science, which he had conceived and nurtured within himself, had suddenly promoted him to the rank of intelligent, programmable objects, relegated to the shelf of objects devoid of special value. The lofty image he had built up of himself was suddenly disturbed. In his body, in the workings of his brain, in the societies and civilizations he had built, man felt a profound metamorphosis taking place. A new version of *Homo sapiens was* emerging in the river of evolution. A brand-new version of man, a potential hybrid, endowed with a different, augmented, connected intelligence, woven into an organic fabric, a skin of communication. A cellular man, the thinking molecule of a brain larger, wider and more powerful than himself. A new man, fragile and strong at the same time, tending towards a tragic hope of superhuman proportions.

1. Creative genesis

The modern vision most of us have of the origin of life is, at heart, rather poetic. It describes the spectacle of billions of billions of particles cruising and playing billiards in the immense space of the universe, and one day getting together to assemble an object with a particular property; an unheard-of event then occurs that resonates in the astral void. This event is the ability of an object to reproduce itself or, more precisely, the ability to *replicate* itself, i.e. to use whatever is within its reach to make an exact copy - apart from a few minor errors inevitable in any reproduction - of the entity just born. Life, if we try to define it in terms of our current knowledge, is the phenomenon by which complex molecules assemble, draw matter and energy from their environment and reproduce. From this microcosmic point of view, we must immediately abandon the long-established idea that the genesis of life is the prologue to man. We need to get rid of the illusion that we are the culmination of an evolutionary process, a chain of transformations of earlier, primitive life forms devoid of any intelligence. We are not a species apart, sovereign and indispensable. In the last twenty years or so, fossil evidence of primitive microbial life, the decoding of DNA and research into human cells have turned all our preconceived ideas about the origin of life and the dynamics of evolution on their head.

In 1986, William Schopf of the University of California, Los Angeles, discovered traces of the first living organisms in geological formations in Western Australia[1] dating back 3.5 billion[2] years. These primitive organisms, born at the bottom of lakes and lagoons, are likely to correspond to what would later become bacteria and algae. These first forms of life, whose relics are engraved in limestone or siliceous rock layers (stromatolites), were extremely rudimentary; they were only a foretaste of the more complex forms that would soon emerge, but they already included a number of subjects greater than the number of human beings that have ever existed. For a long time mysterious and considered rudimentary, it was only very recently that advances in molecular biology revealed that these living organisms lurking in the depths of the ages are not so rustic as all that; they possess an eminently complex character. They are the building blocks of life, still present and indispensable in all living structures on this planet. The most archaic living cell is not a simple heap of molecules, assembled more or less at random; it's a structure that functions according to a *plan*.

The stromatolites of which we find geological traces were made by colonies of cyanobacteria[3] belonging to the class of "prokaryotes". In the archaic dawn of their existence, these organisms, so primitive that they had not yet managed to confine their DNA to the nucleus of a single cell, had nevertheless learned to organize themselves according to a plan, dividing up their functions among other things. Some members of these colonies were in charge of photosynthesis, storing solar energy in specific molecules; others extracted from their environment the substances they needed to feed themselves and disposed of potentially

---

1. They are also found in South Africa, Greenland and the United States.
2. Planet Earth is thought to have formed 4.5 billion years ago. Some scientists believe that life did not appear until 500 million years after the Earth's formation, probably in the depths of the oceans, around underwater hot springs.
3. Cyanobacteria or cyanophyceae are also known as *blue-green algae*. These prokaryotes are widespread in soils, oceans and fresh waters, and are capable of colonizing particularly hostile habitats such as deserts or very warm waters.

toxic waste in landfill sites. Finally, another group was destined to feed on this waste to avoid contamination of other members of the colony. All these interdependent organisms built a generally circular shelter to house them. The architecture of these constructions is considerable considering the microscopic size of these organisms: the edifices sometimes reach and exceed two meters in length. The fossilized remains of these stromatolites are undeniable evidence of organized life: they are built in undulations around a precise center. This form is characteristic of organisms pursuing a strategy of exploration and conquest for food that is found in a large number of bacterial species. James A. Shapiro is considered one of the world's leading authorities on molecular biology, and has aptly titled one of his scientific publications *Bacteria Are Small But Not Stupid*. In it, he demonstrates that modern molecular biology has uncovered "a vast realm of complex intracellular machinery, signal transduction, regulated networks and sophisticated control processes[4]" that were completely unimagined when life was first researched. Indeed, whole generations of scientists have regarded bacteria as uninteresting organisms, solitary cells battling it out in the merciless jungle of microscopic entities. Not so. Even the most primitive bacteria are equipped with information systems and perform a social function: communication.

The latest research shows that the earliest communities of bacteria had developed the very first forms of what we would today call, in anthropomorphic shorthand, "connected intelligence". Indeed, from the very beginning, these primitive living organisms had forged genuine communication links between themselves, using a variety of signalling means - chemical, genetic, physical - capable of broadcasting messages over long distances. All this relatively sophisticated

---

4. SHAPIRO (James A.), "Bacteria are small but not stupid: Cognition, natural genetic engineering, and sociobacteriology", paper published at the conference *Dimensions philosophiques et sociales de la microbiologie*, University of Exeter, July 2006.

machinery, this "creative survival network[5]", fulfilled a primordial objective: to observe the environment in order to warn of dangers, detect opportunities, feed on them and prosper. Bacterial creativity was skillfully expressed in the mastery of attraction and repulsion signals. When the environment around them was sterile or hostile, they emitted appropriate signals to their fellow creatures. Bacteria venturing into the *terrae incognitae* of their environment tagged it with chemical information extremely precious for their survival and growth. From the very beginnings of life, the first organisms were already manipulating information. What's more, in the face of the ever-changing and dangerous world around them, the "genetic engineering" of these micro-organisms was to prove a formidable machine for adaptation and expansion.

Just over 1 billion years after the appearance of the first prokaryotic bacteria, fossil biochemistry detects the appearance of new, more elaborate forms of life[6]. New generations of micro-organisms appeared; unlike their ancestors, they had a nucleus inside the cell, protected by a thin membrane. The proliferation of cellular cooperation could at last begin. Life's evolution towards ever greater complexity began its long journey. These new organisms, the eukaryotes, not only had a nucleus containing the bulk of their genetic material, but also a number of functional accessories[7], chief among them the mito-chondria. Mitochondria are the cell's powerhouses, enabling it to "breathe". The differences between prokaryotes and eukaryotes are fundamental and numerous. This is not the place to describe them. What is at issue is the transition between the two types of organism. How did we get from the elementary prokaryotic organism to the much more complex eukaryote? Some researchers believe that the

---

5. Cf. BEN-JACOB (Eshel) and LEVINE (Herbert), "The Artistry of Nature", in *Nature* n° 409, 2001.
6. At least 2.7 billion years ago.
7. Biologists call them organelles.

transition from one to the other took place gradually, through the creation of specialized compartments within the micro-organism's cytoplasm. The time required for this evolution probably lasted several million years. But there is no trace of any intermediate stages. This is why another theory, developed mainly by the famous microbiologist Lynn Margulis, evokes the very singular idea of co-evolved microbial communities[8]. According to this theory, eukaryotes were originally prokaryotic bacteria that developed a very special sense of hospitality to which we, all living beings on this planet, are eminently indebted: certain bacteria welcomed other organisms as permanent hosts, within their own organism. From these 3-billion-year-old visitors would have derived the various organelles - such as mitochondria - that we find today in the cells of our human bodies[9]. These organisms lived in symbiosis, i.e., in association, with one providing the energy derived from oxygen, another taking responsibility for recycling waste, all in an exchange contract for room and board. Lynn Margulis has no hesitation in saying that "we human beings are the result of a cooperative dynamic between bacteria[10]." Cooperation is thus inscribed at the very heart of our cells, as we now know that many symbioses are hereditarily transmitted[11]. Our human body is witness to this multi-microbial symbiosis, and contains the history book of life on earth in each of its cells.

---

8. This is the theory of serial endosymbiosis.

9. The human body is made up of 10^{16} (10 million billion) animal cells and 10^{17} (100 million billion) bacterial cells.

10. MARGULIS (Lynn) and SAGAN (Dorion), *L'Univers bactériel: les nouveaux rapports de l'homme et de la nature*, Albin Michel, 1989.

11. This is easily observed in certain paramecia (*Paramecium bursaria*), but also in intra-cellular bacteria housed in a small cicada (*Eucelis incisus*), providing it with cholesterol and certain amino acids that the cicada cannot synthesize but which are necessary for its survival. Cf. MARGULIS (Lynn), *Symbiosis in Cell Evolution. Life and Its Environment on the Early Earth*, New York, Freeman, 1981.

Eukaryotes are therefore probably well-integrated, "co-evolved" microbial communities. They are made up of organisms living in an environment that is itself a living organism. The fossil record shows that these organelles gradually evolved into accessories adapted to the environment in which they evolved. Some developed external shells and the ability to move through water, or to crawl thanks to microtubules that contracted or released two shell segments. Others developed vesicles that pumped out external water and released only part of it[12], enabling them to increase their size and capacity[13]. Thanks to this *collaborative effort*, countless stages of mutation and metamorphosis were set in motion, paving the way for the diversity of forms that life on earth would take. Microscopic observation of human cells betrays this eukaryotic secret. Human beings, like all beings made of cells with nuclei, are probably combinations - "chimeras" - from the fusion of previously different and separate creatures. Our nerve cells contain microtubules, descendants of spirochetes, whose role is not clearly established[14] ; sperm cells have whip-like microtubules resembling the flagella of certain bacteria. The proteins that make them up are very similar to those of certain bacteria that have the ability to move at very high speeds. These examples are relics of the symbiotic organization of living organisms.

The genesis I have just briefly described could not have taken place without the networking of independent organisms and the formation of a system for capturing, storing and disseminating information. The first prokaryotic organisms we know, such as cyanobacteria, already possessed, 3.5 billion years ago, the ability to collect and transmit sensory molecules enabling them to avoid danger or take advantage of an opportunity offered by the environment. But the eukaryote

---

12. This is probably the distant prototype of our kidney.
13. Cf. MARGULIS (Lynn) & DOLAN (Michael F.), *Early Life: Evolution on the Precambrian Earth*, Jones & Bartlett Publishers, Sudbury - Massachusetts, 2001.
14. I'll come back to this in Chapter 7 of this book.

was a much larger and more complex organism than its prokaryotic ancestor[15]. Its means of communication was its cytoskeleton which, by changing shape instantaneously, adapted the organism to its environment. These movements were controlled by chemical messengers[16] which carried information from the outside to targets inside the cell. These messages also triggered reactions in the flagella and filaments with which these organisms were equipped, enabling them to flee or move with precision. The prototype of a nervous system was thus in gestation. At the same time, intelligent molecules - genes - were being assembled into a twisted rope - the chromosome. The genes knotted on this rope functioned together in a veritable cooperative system; these assemblies would give rise to massive, dense megamolecules, which eukaryotes would house in a protected nucleus, a veritable central database, which we know today as the genome. Eukaryotes developed ever larger and more complex genomes, paving the way for the diversity of living organisms.

In the early days, cells clustered together in gooey clusters of giant cells containing billions of nuclei, forming fantastic landscapes teeming with life. If you were able to borrow a vehicle to travel back in time, I'd advise you to make a stopover around the beginning of the Proterozoic era (some 1.3 billion years ago). The world you'd discover would be flat and soggy. In the distance, you'd glimpse the smoke plumes of a few volcanoes, and in the foreground, a patchwork of shallow but richly colored pools. On their surfaces, carpets of green and brown foam float gently down to the horizon. This foam coats the riverbanks, tinting the water a rusty color. It clings to the rocks, insinuating itself into the smallest cracks, penetrating the rock itself. If you were equipped with a microscope, you'd see a kaleidoscopic

---

15. The eukaryote was tens or even thousands of times larger than the prokaryotes of the previous stage.
16. Such as cyclic AMP (adenosine monosphate).

world of bubbling purple, aquamarine, red and yellow spheres. Long filaments seem to extend beyond the colorful clusters, creeping slowly toward the sunlight. Tiny organisms wave their whips, while others gather like a light fabric, floating and undulating with the current. Pebbles, boulders and the smallest pebbles are enveloped in vivid reflections of red, pink, yellow and emerald green[17].

Life was teeming, but other innovations were needed to exchange information between these clumped cells. A wiring of microtubules was gradually woven, enabling nerve cells to coordinate every cell in the body. The prototypes of our neural components were emerging. The evolution of these multi-cellular organisms would last 1.2 billion years. But early in the process, the first exotic multi-cellular beings began to appear. As cell networks grew ever more complex, they created ever larger organisms, endowed with the strangest and most varied talents, constantly increasing their capacities as complex information systems. The conquest of terra firma was about to begin. This new adventure called for extraordinarily complex engineering, comparable perhaps to that of our space conquests. Emigrating to land meant modifying all the organ systems of these living beings to adapt them to their new environment. No longer supported by their original aquatic environment, they needed muscles and bone structure to support their weight; they also needed a respiratory system capable of functioning in a gaseous environment with a high oxygen content. These animals needed an outer covering, a scaphander in the form of skin or carapace, to protect them from the dangerous ultraviolet rays of the scorching sun. Their greatest danger was drying out, so they had to carry with them the vital water from the ocean that had been

---

17. Renowned photographer Yann Arthus-Bertrand photographed the *Grand Prismatic Spring* in Yellowstone National Park (Wyoming, USA). In its warm waters, this thermal pool is home to bacterial populations that form a colorful landscape identical to that which the beginnings of our planet must have offered. Cf. ARTHUS-BERTRAND (Yann), *La Terre vue du ciel*, Éditions La Martinière, 1999, p. 18-19.

their habitat. We retain traces of these heroic moments in our own bodies[18]. Human blood has the same salinity as that of the oceans; our sweat and tears are the memory of this extraordinary adventure, when we had to carry the vital sea with us.

This adaptation to the environment in which organisms live is the key to life on earth. Migration to terra firma required the expression of extraordinary genetic engineering to enable life to continue, evolve and develop unceasingly. This effort was not unprecedented; a few hundred million years earlier, life had already had to adapt to cope with the greatest environmental catastrophe, on a planetary scale, that life had ever encountered. The work of micro-organisms at that time not only shaped life, but the biosphere as a whole, in a decisive way, right up to the present day.

Around 2 billion years ago, oxygen pollution caused such genocide that life was forced to evolve or disappear from the planet's surface[19]. At that time, the Earth's atmosphere contained a very low level of oxygen, making it closer to an unknown planet than to the Earth we know today. The micro-organisms that populated it had made hydrogen their main food, which they consumed bulimically, without moderation. A shortage was to be feared, given the scale of consumption. New sources of this precious fuel had to be found. The main hydrogen deposits are to be found in water, which is abundant on our planet. However, the two hydrogen atoms had to be separated from the oxygen atom that makes up a water molecule. After many attempts over several million years, the cyanobacteria of the time succeeded in this feat, inventing and implementing veritable chemical factories powered by solar energy. Having succeeded in breaking down the water molecule, they solved the hydrogen crisis forever. Recovered hydrogen was mixed with carbon dioxide from the air to produce

---

18. *Cf.* Margulis (Lynn), *The Bacterial Universe, op. cit.*
19. I borrow this account from Lynn Margulis, in her *Univers bactériel, op. cit.*

organic foods such as sugars. In this way, life multiplied tenfold and spread more widely than ever before, in jubilant progress.

However, consuming the hydrogen in water inevitably led to the mass release of a waste product: oxygen gas. And while this gas is vital for us today, it was highly toxic for the organisms of the time. This deadly poison escaped in large bubbles from bacterial mats and abundantly polluted even the smallest ponds and streams. When oxygen reacted with organic matter, it attracted electrons and created free radicals - highly reactive chemical substances that literally exploded in micro-organisms. During this period, the oxygen content of the atmosphere rose from 0.0001% to 21%. It was the greatest environmental crisis the Earth had ever known. Many living species were decimated en masse. A giant holocaust threatened all life on earth with nuclear microexplosions. Yet, in the midst of this disaster, resistant bacteria appeared. Indeed, from the very first threat of the deadly gas, the replication of these organisms' genes created protective mechanisms through mutation. These genes contained information that would prove indispensable in adapting to the earth's new atmosphere. The innovations duplicated by the genes spread rapidly throughout the reorganizing microcosm. Genetic engineering reached its apogee when cyanobacteria invented a metabolic system that did not seek to engage in an uncertain war against deadly oxygen, but instead *required it* to function. Life's rescue was to come from the substance that had been its mortal enemy. The new mechanism was aerobic respiration, i.e. the system which, by inhaling oxygen, channels and exploits the reactivity of this gas. The respiration mechanism is a controlled combustion that breaks down organic molecules, rejects carbon dioxide and water, and releases an immense amount of energy. By inventing this oxygen dynamo, the microcosm transformed life and its terrestrial habitat forever. Today, the atmospheric oxygen content is stabilized at 21%; this balance with the environment, from which we all benefit, is a pact made by living beings several hundred million years ago.

Interlude I

The lesson of Jonah

The complex organization found in the most primitive forms of life reveals, from the very beginning, the tension of each living entity between being and non-being; this tragic tension is the hallmark of life, and already carries within itself a horizon of transcendence. The philosopher Hans Jonas believes that "in the obscure movements of organic substance at the origins of the cosmos, there emerges for the first time, within the ever-expanding necessity of the physical universe, the glimmer of a *principle of freedom* - foreign to suns, planets and atoms[20]." Israeli microbiologist Eshel Ben-Jacob is no different when he writes that, by forming organized colonies, the most primitive bacteria "increase the degree of freedom[21] " not only of each individual organism, but also of the community as a whole. The emergence of life would then consist in a relationship of independence, a split between living substance and matter. Life confronts the world in the tension Jonas evokes between being and non-being, between life and death.

---

20. JONAS (Hans), *Evolution and Freedom*, Payot & Rivages, 2000. (Emphasis added).
21. Cf. BEN-JACOB (Eshel), "Bacterial Self-Organization: Co-Enhancement of Complexication and Adaptability in a Dynamic Environment", in *Philosophical Transactions of the Royal Society*, vol. 361, no. 1807, June 15, 2003.

The fundamental layer of every living organism - metabolism, in other words, that which enables relationships with the environment, with the outside world - this primordial and essential function is already a first form of freedom. This idea is not self-evident: how can a chemical process, born in the primordial soup of the cosmos, be the source of a principle such as freedom? By highlighting the relationship between the living organism and its environment, metabolism also reveals the tragically conditional and revocable nature of all life. It is a reality to be achieved, a battle to be waged relentlessly against its opposite. The living organism is summoned to realize its own function in the face of the otherness of matter. To put it another way, in the metabolic process, the organism needs matter, but transforms it for its own sake, thus manifesting a form of "freedom in need[22]". The fundamental freedom of the living organism consists in the independence of form from its own material. The growth of this freedom, this independence from matter, is the very driving force behind the evolution of life.

---

22. JONAS (Hans), *Evolution and Freedom, op. cit.*

2. Information,
the internal structure of the universe

The first forms of life on Earth probably date back just under 4 billion years, but it wasn't until 1944 that one of the first scientific descriptions of the basic model of life was sketched out. This attempt came not from a biologist, but from a physicist, Erwin Schrödinger, the founding father of quantum mechanics; in 1944, he published a small book with the simple but ambitious title: What *is life?* As you'd expect from a physicist, Schrödinger constructs his explanation according to the laws of chemistry and physics. But, in a dazzling stroke of intuition, he realized that the foundations of the chemistry and physics of life hinge on a long-ignored but crucial notion: *information*. And it is information that makes life unique. In his view, not only does life "extract order from its environment[23]", but by mastering its memorization and transmission, it also passes on the genetic code from generation to generation. Some fifty years after the publication of this book, American biologist and physicist Tom Stonier completed and developed Schrödinger's intuition. In his view, matter, energy and information are inextricably linked, as all three are factors in the evolution and organization not only of life, but of

---

23. SCHRÖDINGER (Erwin), *What is Life?* (1944), Seuil, 1993.

the universe as a whole. Living organisms in general, and humans in particular, are expressions of the natural evolution of matter, energy *and* information. For Stonier, humans are "evolved informational systems" whose evolution began as early as the *big bang*. This idea represents a veritable conceptual revolution. The American physicist John Wheeler, one of Einstein's collaborators and the author of numerous works in theoretical physics - it was he who coined the term *black holes* - expresses this radical change in perspective in the sciences of the universe remarkably well: "We see the dawn of a new era, the third era of physics. The first physics was that of motion: Galileo's parabola and Kepler's ellipse; the second was that of law, without any explanation of the law: Newton's laws of motion, Maxwell's electrodynamics, Einstein's geometrodynamics, modern chromodynamics, unification theory and string theory. The third physics is information-based physics[24]." Information was not invented by humans, any more than matter was. Stonier asserts: "Information exists. It doesn't need to be perceived or even understood. It requires no intelligence to interpret it. It doesn't have to have the means to exist. It exists[25]."

Certainly, but we can legitimately ask the question: what is information? Is information something physical or abstract, a material substance or something immaterial? This question has dogged philosophy for as long as it has existed, ever since the Greeks; it has produced entire libraries of reflections, suppositions, hypotheses and theories. For a long time, the scientific community joined common sense in thinking that information was an abstraction. Yet we know, and this is particularly true in biology, that information is always transferred from one replicator to another. It is transmitted from a sender to a

---

24. WHEELER (John A.), "World as System Self Synthesized by Quantum Networking", in *IBM Journal of Research and Development*, vol. 32, January 1988, pp. 4-15.
25. STONIER (Tom), *Information and the Internal Structure of the Universe*, New York, Springer-Verlag, 1990.

receiver, from a "parent" organism to a "child" organism. If information really is an immaterial entity, how can it be inherited as an abstraction? There's a paradox here, because when I tell you the time, for example, I'm communicating information, but I'm not losing it. On the other hand, if I give you my watch, it's obvious that I won't have it on my wrist anymore. Common sense seems to corroborate the idea that information is not an object, a thing, but that it is indeed of an abstract, immaterial nature. Our common sense is thus in line with Cartesian dualism, which saw mind on one side and matter on the other. Information would therefore be on the side of the mind. Information thus possesses a specific quality that matter does not, and is situated in a conceptual universe other than that of physics.

Information is the domain of physics, but it is of a *different* physical nature than matter or energy, because it is at the heart of matter and energy; it is in them, it is a quality or property. Without information, matter and energy would be unstructured, randomly distributed in space. Without information, life would not exist. Information is not located in our usual time, our real time, that of the moment; it's located in another time, virtual or semantic, or imaginary, however we want to call it. In mathematics, we would call it a *topological invariant*, i.e. an organization, a zero point, capable nonetheless of fluctuating between equilibrium and transformation into energy.

To understand Stonier's hypothesis and the special nature of information, we need to turn to a particularly complex concept: entropy, discovered by Rudolf Clausius in the mid-19th century. According to the second principle of thermodynamics, entropy measures the degree of disorder of a system, its quantity of uncertainty; the more disordered the elements of the system, the greater the consumption or misuse of energy. Energy is always present, but it is less concentrated and less available. Entropy, to simplify and avoid scientific language, is everything that degrades, weakens, ages and tends towards perfect order, which for us living beings means death. Yet life is precisely the struggle against entropy. This vital struggle against entropy is made possible by information, which is essentially *negentropic in nature.* In fact, what characterizes life is its activity and above all its reactivity, its capacity to reproduce and cope with the unexpected, to maintain its identity despite external aggression. Life must therefore draw energy from its environment - which is why we need to feed ourselves - to fight entropy and carry out the ceaseless work of repair and exploration, but it is information that guides its action and makes it effective. Indeed, according to Stonier, information possesses recursive properties, i.e. properties that enable it to react to changes in a system's state of equilibrium. Stonier notes that the more complex a system, the greater the probability of state changes and oscillations. The more numerous and complex the changes of state, the greater the growth of information, which can reach exponential rates. The evolution of the universe is an illustration of this principle. At the time of the *big bang*, entropy was gigantic, close to infinity, while information was virtually non-existent[26]. But very quickly, the information content of the universe begins to increase as the system undergoes its first changes of state. Indeed, from the initial explosion, the first change of state occurs: four physical forces are differentiated: gravitation, weak and strong nuclear forces and electromagnetism. Then matter appeared, taking on increasingly complex forms. After some ten billion years, the Earth was born. Then the first forms of life, right up to today's humans. The logic of entropy would have us believe that the universe thus formed is slowly heading towards an inevitable thermodynamic death. However, the concept of an increase in information during

---

26. Theories about what happens before the Big Bang are still controversial and uncertain. Some of them, however, evoke the idea that, at this "instant zero", entropy is zero and information is therefore infinite. This instant zero would be the moment of pure information, outside real time and space. Cf. TOFFOLI (Tommaso) & MARGOLUS (Norman), *Cellular Automata Machines. A New Environment for Modeling*, Cambridge, MIT Press, 1987 and WOLFRAM (Stephen), *A New Kind of Science*, Wolfram Media, 2002.

the evolution of the universe runs counter to the probability of this destiny. Life, thanks to the information that structures it, is a struggle against entropy. Without information, life would be impossible. This is a new approach with profound significance for understanding the development of life in general, and of human beings in particular.

The ordinary objects of physical science, whether protons, molecules or simple stones, all obey a fundamental law of the universe: they're here. And they are here to stay, from all eternity, or at least until the end of their world. These objects are identical to themselves in the unfolding of time, without having to struggle to maintain their identity. The conservation of matter is pure immobility, and not the affirmation, moment by moment, of any identity. The quartz we observe under the microscope is composed of the same particles as in its most distant past; its organization is beautiful, but immobile. Life, on the other hand, from the most elementary micro-organism to the most complex animal, possesses a distinctive characteristic of matter: metabolism, i.e. the constant exchange of information with the environment, which is incorporated, used and then retransmitted. The unique characteristic of living matter is the power to extract information from the world, a power that has its downside: the constraint of always using it, on pain of loss and death.

We now know that not only life in general, but also the evolution of living organisms is closely correlated with changes in the state of their environment. The evolutionary process is the result of an exchange of information between the organism and its environment. This idea, which places information at the very heart of evolution, comes after a long period of controversy. Some have argued that evolution occurs, at the level of genes, through mutations and selections induced by "chance and necessity[27]". Others dismissed the deterministic factor and considered that evolution simply took place through the randomness

27. MONOD (Jacques), *Le Hasard et la Nécessité*, Seuil, 1970.

of mutations and the natural selection of the fittest. It's only fairly recently that some scientists, including the renowned paleontologist Stephen Jay Gould, have come to the view that mutations and the evolution of species are triggered by reactions to environmental changes. In his view, evolution proceeds by alternating long phases of quasi-stagnation with brief periods of "revolutionary" transition, during which extraordinary diversity emerges. This sudden creative and vital energy would be released during[28] phenomena, which would generate major climatic changes[29] and provoke mass extinctions of living species, followed by a profusion of new species.

For a long time, mankind believed that the essence of the universe was matter. And that everything was just matter. Life would have arisen spontaneously from matter; matter containing within itself sufficient energy and vital force to create the spark of life. In ancient China, bamboos were thought to give rise spontaneously to aphids. Sacred Indian writings mention the spontaneous birth of flies from garbage and sweat. Babylonian inscriptions record that canal mud could give rise to worms. In ancient Egypt, it was thought that the silt deposited by the Nile could spontaneously generate frogs and toads[30]. For Greek philosophers such as Thales, Democritus, Epicurus, Lucretius and even Plato, life is the very property of matter; it is eternal and appears spontaneously whenever the conditions are right. These ideas, synthesized by Aristotle, endured through the Middle Ages and the Renaissance, and were supported by eminent thinkers such as Newton, Descartes and Bacon. Even Buffon, in the middle of the 18th century, asserted that nature is full of life germs capable of scattering during decay, then uniting to produce microbes. It wasn't until Louis

---

28. Like meteorite falls, for example.
29. *Cf.* GOULD (Stephen Jay), *The Structure of Evolutionary Theory*, Gallimard, 2006.
30. *Cf.* BRACK (André) & RAULIN (François), *L'Évolution chimique et les origines de la vie*, Dunod, 1997.

Pasteur changed his mind and put an end to these misconceptions. On June 22, 1864, he demonstrated that it was germs in the ambient air that altered aqueous solutions, thus underpinning the theory that ambient matter could not generate a new, organized being devoid of parents. By demonstrating that life can only originate from pre-existing living beings, Pasteur opened the door to new mysteries - those of the beginning of life, its replication and evolution.

For as long as it was believed that the essence of the universe was matter alone, life could only be described by its visible organization. Life was seen as a kind of model capable of leaving an imprint on the surface of reality, but one that could be lost in future generations. The idea of matter as the foundation of life petrified and sterilized any possibility of envisaging other models for the development of living things. This thinking was certainly at the root of the emergence of normative thinking, structuralism and fundamentalism in the religious sphere[31]. Correlatively, the notion of energy was seen to introduce the entropic dimension, with the bleak prospect of inevitable thermal death. This vision probably contributed to the cynical currents of thought that developed at the end of the nineteenth and especially in the twentieth century, and which are not without responsibility for the unprecedented ferocity of this period of history, nor for the wanton and reckless destruction of the planet by human activity.

The emergence, in addition to matter and energy, of the notion of information as a fundamental structure of the universe, nature and life opens up considerable potential in our appreciation of life, consciousness and human development in its natural environment. Life is not just a matter of selecting the strongest or the best adapted; consciousness is an abundance of possibilities, cooperative relationships, exchanges, intelligence and creative networks. The infor-

---

31. Cf. Rossi (Ernest), "What is life? L'évolution de l'information du flux quantique au Soi", in *Perspectives psychologiques*, n° 26, pp. 6-22, 1992.

mation systems that mankind has begun to set up barely approach, in their scope, those of living organisms, whose smallest organisms share and exchange information and a memory rich in billions of years of continuous functioning.

Theories of information and consciousness are now enriched by the contributions of quantum physics. The field of research is immense, mysterious and still uncertain, but, in this field, "subtle and unexpected answers[32]" can emerge at any moment. I'll tell you more about Roger Penrose's work on the brain in a later chapter, and you'll see that some of his hypotheses leave you dreaming. Quantum theories of information are turning Shannon's classical scheme on its head: information can no longer be reduced to "bits". It's not just a signal, it's also meaning. It unfolds outside time and space, becoming "hyperinformation[33]" and opening up perspectives in which the role of humans is central, as observers and players in a global consciousness of the world.

---

32. CHARPAK (Georges) & OMNÈS (Roland), *Soyez savants, devenez prophètes*, Odile Jacob, 2004.

33. I introduced this theme in *La Grande Confusion*, France Europe Éditions, 2006; I'll develop it further in chapter 10.

Interlude II

The dance of the bee

In the course of their evolution, little by little, the honeybees we frequently encounter on a fine summer's day have developed a particularly sophisticated communication system that defies imagination. To share their knowledge and inform their fellow bees of the exact location of a territory rich in honey flowers... they dance. Not just any dance. A highly codified, *intelligent* dance[34].

Sometimes, on one of her expeditions, a bee comes across a superb field of flowers, a veritable vein of food. Intoxicated with pollen and nectar, she's certainly not going to keep this secret to herself. Her nature as a bee makes her an integral part of collective life. So she has to share her secret with the other bees in her hive. Returning from her expedition, laden with pollen, she enters the darkened hive. The other bees go about their business. Our traveler bee then sets about attracting their attention by starting a frenetic round. Her fellow bees gather round, very excited, because they've understood that this round

---

34. This observation is recounted by Richard DAWKINS IN his book *Qu'est-ce que l'évolution? The River of Life*, Hachette Littératures, 1997. He refers to the remarkable book by Karl von, *The Dance Language and Orientation of Bees*, Leigh E. Chadwick, Cambridge, Harvard University Press, 1967, French translation, *Vie et mœurs des abeilles*, Albin Michel, 1984.

means there's food not far away, in the immediate vicinity of the hive. So far, so good.

When the food is far from the hive, however, the dance becomes much more interesting. The bee in possession of the precious information begins to wriggle and move curiously along the vertical face of the hive comb. As the interior of the hive is dark, the bees can't see the dancer's movements; instead, they feel and hear the rhythmic sounds that accompany the bee's dance. This dance follows the shape of a figure eight, with a straight axis down the middle. We understand that this straight line serves to indicate the direction in which the food is located. At this stage, we can imagine that the bee is using a fairly simple indicator to signify a direction, just as we do when we point our index finger in a certain direction. In reality, it's much more complicated. The bee dances along the vertical wall of the hive. So the axis of the figure-of-eight dance doesn't really mean the direction to take. Rather, the bee seems to be using the wall of the hive, as if a staff map were pinned to it. But the direction indicated on this virtual map is not enough to understand the information the bee wants to convey. A reference point is needed, and that reference point is the sun. During the course of their evolution, bees have assimilated the fact that the top of the hive - i.e. the top of the "map" - represents the direction towards the sun. The bottom indicates a direction away from the sun. Between these two points, the bee identifies a number of intermediate positions, just as we do with the degrees of a compass. The direction given by the bee is therefore very precise in relation to the position of the sun. But this direction is still insufficient, as it does not give the distance to the food. To transmit this additional, but essential, information, the dancing bee imparts a highly calculated rhythm to its wriggling. The slower the rhythm, the greater the distance. The faster the dance, the closer the food is to the hive.

The bees grouped around the dancer listen and feel this dance; they measure the rhythm of the wriggling and certainly the speed of rotation; they measure the angle made by the axis of the figure eight of the dance in relation to the vertical; once the message is "understood", they leave the hive and head straight in the direction given, in search of their precious nectar. Their line of flight is at exactly the same angle to the sun as that indicated by the dancing bee to the vertical of the hive comb. The duration of their flight is inversely proportional to the logarithm of the dancer bee's wriggling speed. To communicate their information, bees not only know spatial geometry, they also know how to calculate logarithms! Needless to say, bees in the southern hemisphere do the same dance, but in reverse.

3. The digital logic of life

On the very first page of his famous book *La Logique du vivant*, François Jacob writes: "Today, heredity is described in terms of information, messages and code[35]." This sentence, written in 1970, seems to be a commonplace in biology today. However, in the context of living organisms, this assertion contains an obscure zone that lies at the heart of the notion of information. In a seminal article published in 1948, Claude Shannon proposed a definition of information that seems set in stone: what characterizes information is its improbability[36]. For Shannon, who was an engineer at the *Bell Telephone Company*, information is considered "data" in every sense of the word, in the most mathematical sense of an object to be processed, and in the sense of immediate and certain accessibility. In this engineering approach, the focus is on the probability of a message appearing. In other words, when the probability of an item of information is high, its informative value tends towards zero. The more unlikely a message is, the greater its information value. According to this logic, an information system is necessarily based on an ordered set of variations. The American anthropologist Gregory Bateson uses a pretty formula to describe this

---

35. JACOB (François), *La Logique du vivant*, Gallimard, 1970.
36. Cf. SHANNON (Claude E.), "A Mathematical Theory of Communication", *Bell System Technical Journal*, n° 27, 1948.

characteristic: "Information is a difference that makes a difference[37]." To use a more trivial image, information is a ringtone that stands out from ambient noise. For the moment, remember that information is first and foremost a variation. But it's also an *invariance*. While Shannon's strictly technical definition does not concern itself with the meaning of information, with the content of the message, it is clear that information cannot simply be transmitted; it must also be interpreted. To be transmitted, information must be encoded by the sender; but for the receiver to interpret this information, he or she must also possess this code. Both sender and receiver must have the same code. If they don't, the meaning of the message is lost - which, I'm sure you'll agree, is common sense. If we follow this idea, then we must admit that the code is necessarily invariant.

Let's explain: a sender who wants to transmit a message first encodes it. But the encoded message in no way includes the code, let alone its encryption keys. This is impossible for one simple reason: information is variable, whereas the code is invariant; the two notions are necessarily distinct. To understand this essential characteristic, we need only take the example of a coded language such as Morse code[38]. In this language, each letter of the alphabet corresponds to a code: A = •−, B = −•••, C = −•−•, and so on. This is a system in which differences (variations) between letters translate into differences between symbols. The code, on the other hand, is invariant. Let's now try to specify the code within a Morse code signal. Let's send the message that the letter A is equivalent to the code "•−". In Morse code, this would be translated as "the letter •− is equivalent to the sign •−". This is an inoperative tautology that highlights the fact that the code, i.e. the series of signs "•" or "−", is incapable of specifying whether these signs refer to letters

---

37. BATESON (Gregory), *Vers une écologie de l'esprit*, Seuil, 1991.
38. See John STEWART's development of this example in *La vie existe-t-elle? Reconciling Genetics and Biology*, Vuibert, 2004.

of the alphabet or to any other object. The key to the code cannot be transmitted in the information itself; it is necessarily external to the system. A computer can perform prodigious operations, but it only does so because it has been programmed by computer scientists. They have given it the code in the form of a program, so that it can function and process information. Programs are invariants, whereas processed information is a variable. The invariants cannot be set up by the information system itself, because computers are not, until now, made by themselves, but by external systems: the engineers.

In the light of these reflections, François Jacob's sentence opens up an interstice in which metaphysics slyly appears. The question Jacob implicitly poses is whether we can legitimately apply materialistic concepts of code and information to living organisms and, to put it more broadly, to life itself. For if life is characterized by a - genetic - code, where is the program that interprets the code, and who designed it? This question of the metaphysical intervention of a great Architect in the organization of life is not new; it goes back to the dawn of time and still seems inexhaustible. Even today, certain movements evoke an "intelligent design"[39], which would be at the origin of the mysteries of creation and life. This current of thought, which feeds the proselytizing theses of American antiatheists and Muslim religious fundamentalists alike, develops ideas that are both anti-evolutionist and anti-Darwinian[40]. The critical basis is fuelled in particular by the theses published by the English theologian William

---

39. Intelligent Design.

40. A century and a half after the publication of *The Origin of Species*, some countries, notably the United States, have been forced to legislate against the teaching of Darwinian theory or its opponents; European countries are not to be outdone, and are now also faced with the same demands from creationist lobbies. On this subject, see Jacques ARNOULD's interesting investigation, *Dieu versus Darwin. Les créationnistes vont-ils triompher de la science*, Albin Michel, 2007.

Paley in 1802[41]. He used an analogy to prove the existence of God: that of the Watchmaker. This metaphor had been used before him by many authors, including Descartes who, although emblematic of materialism, was profoundly dualist and spiritualist in everything to do with man; the analogy of the Watchmaker tends to explain the structures of the universe by divine intervention. If you look at a clock," says Paley, "you'll notice how each part is finely tuned to the others, so that each fulfills an important function for the whole. It's impossible not to see this as the work of a clockmaker, the only person capable of shaping this mechanism with an overall project in mind. Observing a living being leads to the same conclusion. So, following this logic, we are entitled to conclude that a "divine watchmaker" certainly exists. Some sixty years after the publication of this thesis, Darwin published his research on *The Origin of Species*[42]. The first edition of 1859 makes no mention of the Creator, but in view of the outcry over his book, and despite the fact that his discourse on the origin of man and his societies effectively dispenses with any reference to the transcendent, he slips one in, certainly reluctantly, at the very end of the text of the second edition of 1860. It has to be said that Darwin's theory of evolution is based on an unstable pivot with regard to the notion of information: natural selection is operated according to the mechanism of hereditary variations - of variables. However, the biology of his time was far from having satisfactory theories to explain the functioning of an (invariant) system capable of processing and decoding genetic information (variables)[43] other than by supernatural intervention. It would be more than a

---

41. PALEY (William), *Natural Theology, Evidences of the Existence and Attributes of the Deity (1802)*, Oxford World's Classics, 2006.

42. DARWIN (Charles), *The Origin of Species by Means of Natural Selection (1859)*, La Découverte, 1989.

43. The first theoretical principles of modern genetics and heredity were established by Gregor Mendel in the 1860s.

century before sufficient arguments could be put forward against the Watchmaker analogy.

In 1986, Richard Dawkins published a book entitled *The Blind Watchmaker*, in which he demonstrated that living organisms are complex systems that are produced and evolve according to a succession of small random sequences. Each small step is the result of a random modification of the genetic instructions. Some of these modifications are unfavorable for the organism, and can even kill it. Others, on the contrary, confer a selective advantage, for example in relation to a given environment; in this case, the organism will have more offspring than individuals who have not undergone this modification. The beneficial advantage of the mutation, passed on to descendants, will then spread progressively throughout the population, with each individual possessing the improved version of the gene, while the previous version will be eliminated. No omniscient watchmaker, then, according to Dawkins' theory: "Despite appearances, the only watchmaker in nature is the blind forces of physics, even if they are deployed in quite particular ways[44]." No intelligent design either, for while a true watchmaker anticipates what he is going to do by designing gears and mechanisms assembled according to a goal he has set himself, natural selection is a blind process. "It has no mind, and it has no mind's eye. It doesn't foresee the future. It has no vision, no power of anticipation; it can see nothing. If it can be said to play the role of the watchmaker, then it is a *blind* watchmaker[45]."

Following on from Dawkins' ideas, philosopher Daniel Dennett describes the evolutionary process as an *algorithm*, i.e. a procedure devoid of intelligence, but which must necessarily produce a result when it follows a certain number of precise steps[46]. We are accus-

---

44. DAWKINS (Richard), *The Blind Watchmaker (1986)*, Robert Laffont, 1999.
45. *Ibid.*
46. Cf. DENNETT (Daniel), *Is Darwin dangerous?*, Odile Jacob, 2000.

3. The digital logic of life

tomed, some without realizing it, to manipulating algorithms in our daily lives. The act of 1) putting a coin of a precise amount into the slot of a machine, 2) pressing a button, 3) putting a cup under a spout, 4) waiting and 5) removing the cup, constitutes a sequence of gestures that results in an espresso coffee. If the sequence is not scrupulously followed, particularly step 3, a minor domestic disaster will ensue. Our computers operate on the same principle. Algorithms don't need a hidden mind to work; all they need is for the procedure to be followed. This is why Dennett describes Darwinian evolutionary theory as "a scheme for creating design out of chaos, without the help of the mind". However, this formula could imply that if evolution follows an algorithm, its results should be determined and predictable. But we know that this is not the case, as life takes place within the logic of complex systems. Chaos theory explains that these systems are extremely sensitive to their initial condition, and that a tiny difference in their origin can lead to very different results. Evolution therefore follows a simple algorithm, but being a chaotic system, its outcome is extraordinarily complex and unpredictable. It is impossible to predict the outcome, which is the fruit of a process that only works once and cannot be repeated identically. Stephen Jay Gould states in his book *Life is Beautiful*: "Any unfolding of history, altered by a seemingly insignificant iota at its beginning, would have yielded an equally sensible and totally different outcome, but extremely distasteful to our vanity, since it would not include any self-conscious life... Thousands and thousands of times it has been as little as that (put your thumb about a millimetre from your forefinger) that we have been purely and simply erased from the film of life, following a change of course in history, which would then have taken another equally sensible course[47]." No plan prior to the evolutionary process

---

47. GOULD (Stephen Jay), *La vie est belle*, Seuil, 1991.

could have anticipated the beings we are today, or the world around us. And what we will be tomorrow.

1953 was a great year for life science research. It was the year when two young researchers from Cambridge's Cavendish Laboratory, Francis Crick and James Watson, triggered an immense scientific revolution by discovering, with the DNA double helix, that molecular biology is digital. Since then, we've known that genes, with their sophisticated internal structure, are long strings of digital information. What's more, the genetic code is a unique phenomenon: a veritable language of nature, it translates genes into proteins for all living beings, in the same language.

Genes are digital in the strongest sense of the word, that of computers or CD-Roms. The genetic code is not binary like the computer code, but quaternary, made up of four symbols[48]. Before 1953, it was possible to believe that there was something mysterious, mystical, supernatural or transcendental in living protoplasm. In reality, this can no longer reasonably be the case, as "our genetic system, which is universal for life on our planet, is digital to the core[49]." Genes carry pure information that can be encoded or decoded without degradation and without changing the meaning. Since information is digital by nature, it can be copied indefinitely without loss of quality. It is this digital characteristic that allows DNA characters to be duplicated from one generation to the next with near-absolute precision. Dawkins confronts us with our own reality: "We - that is, all living things - are survival machines programmed to propagate the digital database that made this programming possible. In this new context, Darwinism is the survival of the survivors from the point of view of the pure digital message[50]."

---

48. Genetic information is encoded in the form of a sequence made up of the four nucleotides A, T, C and G in a DNA molecule, which is a biochemical substrate.
49. DAWKINS (Richard), What is *evolution? op. cit.*
50. *Ibid.*

There are three main requirements for natural selection to work. Francis Crick explains that the first requirement is a "vehicle" to house the information. This vehicle is an organism with a process capable of exactly duplicating the information. The second requirement is that the duplication must be capable of producing entities that can themselves be reproduced by the duplication process. Duplication is not a simple reproduction like a photocopy, which can only produce copies of the machine that copied it. The third requirement is that errors - i.e. mutations - must themselves be copied if natural selection is to be able to preserve favorable variations[51].

Genetics is constitutively based on duplication, but also on variations and differences. In all hypotheses, we are in the realm of information variables. But the question remains: what about the invariant? What is the nature of the program - the *software* - that makes these variables work? Chilean biologist Humberto Maturana has based all his research on this question: "What is the invariant characteristic of living systems around which natural selection operates[52]?" To answer this question, it is necessary to conceive of the living system not just as the theory of natural selection does, in reference to its environment or context, but also in reference to itself, as an autonomous unit. Maturana thus develops the idea of "circular organization" to describe living entities, an idea which, once stated, appears self-evident. Indeed, if we ask ourselves what produces a living organism, the answer can be none other than the living organism itself[53]. An animal, plant, micro-organism, organ or tissue is the result of an ongoing process of production and renewal of its constituent molecules. This characteristic is exclusive to living

---

51. *Cf. Crick* (Francis), *A Life to Discover. De la double hélice à la mémoire*, Odile Jacob, 1989.
52. MATURANA (Humberto) & VARELA (Francisco), *Autopoiesis and Cognition: The Realization of the Living*, Springer, 1979.
53. Cf. STEWART (John), *op. cit.*

beings; indeed, a machine produces something other than itself, and is produced by something other than itself. In collaboration with his colleague and compatriot Francisco Varela, Maturana used the term *autopoiesis* to designate this phenomenon of circular organization, i.e. the capacity of a system to produce, maintain and define itself[54]. So, if the variables of the living system are genes, the fundamental invariant is its *organization*, at the very level of the cell. However, this invariant character is not limited to the level of the single-cell organism; it becomes more complex in multicellular living organisms, and is located at the level of ontogeny, i.e. at the very heart of the reproductive process.

The question that arises here can be summed up in the common paradox of the chicken and the egg. The theory of autopoiesis has shown that the cell contains a number of biochemical components, such as nucleic acids and proteins, which structure an organization reduced to a small number of elements, such as the nucleus or the cytoskeleton. Subjected to an external flow of molecules and energy, these structures produce the components which, in turn, maintain the structure's contents and enable its components to grow; we are indeed in a circular system. But how does the ontogeny of a multicellular living organism work? Richard Dawkins tells us[55] that when an embryo begins to form, a single cell (the fertilized egg) divides into two parts. Then each of these two parts divides into four, the four into eight, and so on. In just a few dozen generations, billions upon billions of cells can be produced. What interests us here is that these billions of cells are not all identical; far from it. They differentiate into liver cells, kidney cells, heart cells, eye cells, etc., each with different active genes and enzymes. How is this differentiation possible, how is it "programmed", what is the invariant? To answer

---

54. *Cf.* Varela (Francisco), *Autonomie et connaissance. Essai sur le vivant*, Seuil, 1989.
55. *Cf.* Dawkins (Richard), What *is evolution? op. cit.*

3. The digital logic of life

this question, Dawkins uses the analogy of computer bootstrapping. In the 1960s, long before the advent of PCs, computers were huge machines. Programs and data were stored on punched cards. But it wasn't enough to make the machine swallow packs of punched cards to make it work; it didn't know *a priori* what these cards represented. So the computer had to be "primed" to understand what its mission was, and this was done simply by switching switches in a ritualistic sequence. On today's PCs, computer bootstrapping takes place within the computer itself[56] and takes place as soon as the computer is switched on.

How is a living system "primed"? How do you differentiate the cells that will be formed from a single egg? The answer lies in the egg itself. An egg, i.e. the first cell to divide and form the embryo and then the living being, generally takes the form of a sphere. Its internal chemistry assigns it a polarity: an egg has a top and a bottom, and often a front and a back. These polarities are linked to chemical gradients: certain chemical substances are more concentrated as you move from front to back, and other substances increase according to their position high or low in the egg. These gradients are extremely simple; they exist right from the start, but they are sufficient for priming. When the egg begins to divide, into a few dozen cells, we observe that some cells, which were located at the top of the egg, will have certain chemical substances, while others will have a different dosage from the lower part. These differences activate different combinations of genes in different cells. The cells did not reproduce as clones; they differentiated immediately. At the start of the process, the cells all have the same genes, but as the work of differentiation proceeds, not only do the genes combine in different ways, but the genes themselves can

---

56. On most PCs, this is the Bios (Basic Input Output System), which is loaded each time the computer is started up and contains basic functions and routines stored in the motherboard's ROM.

make some of them active and others inactive. The work continues until the entire repertoire of cells has been built up.

The embryonic process is particularly complex in both physics and chemistry. The slightest modification at any stage of development can have far-reaching consequences. The process is so sensitive that two individuals, even twins, will never be completely identical. In all cases, the differences are essentially due to the genes themselves, but also to the way they interact[57]. This characteristic allows natural selection to operate, and to favor or disfavor certain aspects of the embryo's development process. Remember: when you were still an ape, you walked on all fours, jumping from tree to tree, like most of the gorillas and chimpanzees around you. Then one day, a member of your group stood up on his two hind legs; standing up, he could see further into the dangers of the vast savannah before him. Better armed against its hostile environment, it was able to live longer than the others[58]. Natural selection therefore favored those with an upright posture, because they survived better than the others. Being able to stand upright, to run on two legs, has an effect, however small, on the probability of such an individual surviving to have children and offspring. To the extent that upright posture is a genetic quality, the genes are more likely to be passed on to the next generation[59]. Genes that survive less well will gradually disappear from the river of evolution.

---

57. Genes don't explain all differences. Some are also due to differences in environment.

58. According to paleoanthropologist Yves Coppens, the collapse of the Rift Fault in Africa some 8 million years ago triggered an "ecological break". As the eastern part of the continent dried out, the savannah gained ground on the forest. Our arboreal ancestors adapted to their new environment by standing on their hind legs to watch the horizon. Bipedalism freed their hands and favored brain development. Cf. COPPENS (Yves), *Pré-ambules : les premiers pas de l'homme*, Odile Jacob, 2001.

59. Paleontologist Jean Chaline points out that species evolve in situ through minimal changes: the frequency of genotypes varies, manifested in morphological modifications. These changes do not immediately give rise to new populations, but the descending population is no longer identical to the one that preceded it. Cf. CHALINE (Jean), *What's new since Darwin? La théorie de l'évolution dans tous ses états*, Ellipses, 2006.

From the gene's point of view, the only perspective is a *selfish* one[60]: that of being able to cross generations as best as possible. There is no divine Watchmaker or transcendent Spirit in this perspective: "The presence of the supernatural has ceased to be a given of experience; it is now the exclusive province of illusion[61]."

60. Dawkins (Richard), *The Selfish Gene*, Armand Colin, 1990.
61. Finkielkraut (Alain), *L'Humanité perdue. Essai sur le xxᵉ siècle, Seuil, 1996.*

Interlude III

The kidnapping of Professor Crickson

This story is told by Richard Dawkins[62]. It's a science-fiction theme, although the technology required by the plot is hardly more advanced than what we have today.

Professor Crickson is an internationally renowned biologist. He's been kidnapped by a terrorist organization, locked up and forced to work on an evil project of germ warfare. Humanity is in danger. To save human beings from certain doom, the professor must succeed in communicating a vital piece of information to the outside world. Of course, all means of communication with the outside world are forbidden.

Crickson is not Bruce Willis, but simply a biologist. He knows that the DNA code consists of sixty-four units of code, more than enough symbols for all the letters of the alphabet, ten digits, a space character and punctuation. With Professor Crickson locked away in a bacteriological warfare laboratory, it's easy for him to find a highly virulent virus; there are several available on the shelves. He chooses a particular flu virus and sets about composing, in the virus's genome, the text of a warning message for the whole world. He writes the

____

62. *In Qu'est-ce que l'évolution, op. cit.*

entire text of his message in his best English and repeats it over and over again in the resulting genome, adding a characteristic reference sequence: the first ten numbers. Crickson then injected himself with the virus. A few days later, when his kidnappers are in his laboratory, he sneezes.

Within hours, a flu epidemic swept the planet. Laboratories around the world analyze the new flu virus and set about deciphering the corresponding genome in order to produce an effective vaccine. However, it soon became apparent that the genome contained a foreign repeating sequence.

Intrigued by the presence of numbers arranged in a sequence that has nothing to do with chance, a biologist on the other side of the planet understands that he is in the presence of an encrypted message. Nothing could be easier than to read, as if from an open book, the message that Professor Crickson has been sneezing all over the world.

4. Genes and memes, the same battle

The most recent research into the evolution of living organisms all confirms a conclusion that is not very pleasing to the human *ego*: we are not the main players in the cycle of life. It's an object that we can't observe, that we can only characterize indirectly, and yet which is the seat of life's coded information: the gene. It is not living creatures that make the gene to be passed on to their descendants; it is the gene that makes increasingly sophisticated creatures, in order to ensure *its* own survival. The inversion of perspective is somewhat vexing, but this is the reality of life. Genes select and adapt the most suitable vehicles to provide protection and offspring. To achieve this result, they develop the most extravagant technical tricks, in the face of which we rave in praise of nature's prodigious diversity and inventiveness. Dawkins refers to this new view of life as the *selfish gene*[63]. But the selfish gene is a literary shorthand that can obscure part of the reality: the gene never works alone, it combines with other genes to obtain a result, the fruit of a collaborative effort[64]. So, for example, the genes that promote the digestion of meat are found in all kinds of furry, feathered or scaly creatures. Regardless of their appearance, the key point is that these creatures *also* have genes that determine the presence of strong jaws

---

63. *Op. cit.*
64. Part of this result is the so-called "phenotype".

and possibly sharp teeth. The combination of the two gene categories will lead to the production of a "vehicle" that will be healthier, have a better chance of survival and have numerous offspring.

The gene has one obsession: its transmission, or to be more precise, its *replication*[65]. It is therefore endowed with highly sophisticated physico-chemical equipment enabling it to make highly faithful copies of the molecules from which it is formed. It took billions of years for complex organic molecules[66] capable of copying themselves to appear on our planet. But once invented, the process never stopped.

The question we can legitimately ask ourselves is whether there are entities on our planet other than genes that possess this replication power. We're thinking, of course, of certain proteins or prions, which are still so little known. It's not certain that their replication power, if it exists, is as powerful as that of the gene. This is why Dawkins invites us to take an interest in another replicant, which we have before our eyes, but which we do not distinguish to its full extent. This entity evolves in an environment that usually eludes the life sciences, chemistry or physics, since it is *culture*.

Let's listen to Dawkins speak, for it's rare to see a new field of knowledge opened up in so few words: "Genes and the DNA molecule happen to be the entities capable of replication that prevail on our planet. There may be others. If they exist, provided other requirements are met, they will almost inevitably become the basis of an evolutionary process. Will we have to go to distant worlds to find other kinds of replicators and other kinds of

---

65. In *The Selfish Gene*, Richard Dawkins introduced the term "replicator". This is a primordial entity that is the object of selection. This object has the power, autonomously or through the intermediary of other objects or beings, to reproduce itself identically, apart from variations. The "power to reproduce" is not the same as the simple ability to be reproduced, as it implies a quality of dynamic autonomy. Replicators exist and are of interest only because they have the ability to reproduce themselves *identically*. Considered over time, they are permanent, which does not rule out the possibility of copying errors or *variations*. Species stability depends on the permanence of replicators.
66. These are ribonucleic acid (RNA) and deoxyribonucleic acid (DNA).

52

evolution? I think a new type of replicator has recently appeared on our planet; it's staring us right in the face. It's still a child, moving clumsily through the original soup, but already undergoing evolutionary change at a rate that leaves the old genes staggering and far behind.

The new soup is that of human culture. We need a name for this new replicator, a name that evokes the idea of a unit of cultural transmission or a unit of imitation. Mimème comes from a Greek root, but I prefer a one-syllable word that sounds a bit like gene, so I hope my classicist friends will forgive me for abbreviating mimème to mème[67]."

While genes have been splashing around in the protoplasmic soup since the origin of life, memes have been floating in a different kind of soup, one that appeared later: that of human brains. But what is a meme? As memetics is a relatively recent field (Dawkins' book, which first mentions it, appeared in the USA in 1976), attempts at definition are numerous, sometimes contradictory and often exaggerated in the scope they seek to encompass. The inventor of the word *"meme" didn't* develop his intuition at length. He gives a relatively general definition: a meme is a replicator, the basic unit of cultural information. As examples of memes, he gives melodies, slogans, clothing fashions, ways of making objects, and so on. In order to replicate themselves, memes are propagated from brain to brain by a process which, in a very broad sense, can be called imitation.

Psychologist Susan Blackmore[68], who follows in Dawkins' footsteps, sees the risk of misuse and confusion that an overly broad definition could bring to the discipline. In her view, the meme is inappropriately used to designate an idea or concept, something ethereal and immaterial. She therefore returns to the source, i.e. the brief definition given by Dawkins, which inspired the one recently published

---

67. *Dawkins (Richard), The Selfish Gene, op. cit.*
68. *Cf.* BLACKMORE (Susan), *Meme Theory. Why we imitate each other*, Max Milo, 2006.

by the *Oxford English Dictionary*: "A meme is an element of culture that can be transmitted by non-genetic means, and more particularly by imitation." This means that any unit of information *that is copied* from one person to another is a meme. Every word in the language, every way of speaking, every story we know or every song we hum, is made up of memes. Memes are not just abstractions, they can also be artifacts. The style of our houses, the shape of our bicycles, the design of our streets, the design of our cars are all memes, or forms defined by memes.

Memetics is an extremely recent discipline, at the crossroads of several others, and is the subject of intense research and publication, especially in Great Britain and the United States. In France, the concept of the meme is either ignored or scorned and rejected by the vast majority of sociologists who claim to be influenced by Durkheim and structuralism. French-language works on the subject are rare, which is undeniably a shortcoming in the human sciences[69]. Without getting into a vain Franco-French quarrel about the relevance of memetics and the scope of the meme's definition, and bearing in mind that, in the current state of our knowledge, this concept is not yet of a very stable scientific nature, we can simply retain that the core of its definition is *non-genetic information copied from one person to another.* Consequently, a large part of our culture is made up of memes; on the other hand, everything that goes on in our minds, a *priori,* has nothing to do with memes.

Stop reading this page for two minutes.

Are you back? In two minutes, what ideas, what thoughts went through your head? You've been thinking about the dinner you're going to make tonight, the backfire of the motorcycle that went by in the street, the cat that brushed against your leg. All these incessant

---

69. The only French publication to date is Pascal Jouxtel's *Comment les systèmes pondent. Introduction à la mémétique*, Vuibert, 2005.

thoughts that our brain produces are not memes. We can be extraordinarily moved by the sight of a beautiful landscape or a work of art, and remember it in minute detail, without this involving memes. On the other hand, not all learning involves memes. What we learn on our own, or by trial and error, is not in the realm of memes. What is, however, is learning that corresponds to the acquisition of precise *instructions* reproduced to achieve a desired goal. Many living creatures are capable of extensive learning and teaching, but they don't have memes, because they can't transfer what they've learned to someone else in the form of decomposed instructions. A limited capacity for imitation may exist in birds, dolphins, and probably in some primates. Chimpanzees and orangutans may be capable of more or less rudimentary forms of imitation; but only humans are capable of a certain type of general, widespread imitation that makes a second "replicant" possible and thus determines memetic evolution.

A monkey can learn perfectly well, by imitating one of its little friends, to break a coconut with a stone. Learning by imitation is a long and arduous process, marked by failure and repetition until the right gesture is mastered. In this process, instructions are non-existent or very rudimentary; all you have to do is watch and try to reproduce. There's no guarantee that the gesture will be transmitted in the correct manner; it's even possible to imagine that, after a certain number of copies, the result will be quite different from breaking a coconut. It's not a meme, then, since the copy degrades rapidly and the chances of transmission and evolution are significantly altered.

In *Poetics,* Aristotle asserted: "Man differs from other animals in that he is the most inclined to imitate[70]." Indeed, man seems to be the only animal that can imitate, in the sense of memetic theory, because he is capable of defining instructions - in the same way as an algorithm - in

---

70. ARISTOTLE, *Poetics*, 48b, 6-7, trans. Roselyne Dupont-Roc and Jean Lallot, Seuil, 1980.

which the steps are broken down, analyzed and synthesized for easy reproduction. The example of *origami is* frequently given to illustrate this characteristic. Origami is a paper-folding technique designed to represent an object, usually an animal. The paper casserole is an origami. If you don't know the precise instructions and try to imitate me simply by watching me make it, it will be almost impossible for you to reproduce my paper cocotte correctly. On the other hand, if I tell you to fold the sheet of paper in half, then fold the left-hand corner over the bottom right-hand corner, etc., there's a good chance that, if you follow the step-by-step instructions I've given you, your cocotte will be just as beautiful as mine. A human being can make a paper casserole under these conditions; no other animal can. The set of instructions - that is, the organized sequence of decomposed information - needed to make this origami is called a meme.

Memes spread indiscriminately, whether they are useful or useless, beneficial or harmful. The meme point of view, like that of the gene, is selfish. Genes and memes are replicators that are merely pieces of information, coded in DNA or copied from brain to brain by a process of imitation. They are selfish in the sense that they are copied whenever possible or when environmental conditions are right. In the case of memes, they will direct our behavior in order to achieve maximum replication, regardless of the impact of this process on us, our genes, our environment or our planet.

Like genes, memes like to work collectively; they are selected in relation to other memes in the same memetic *pool.* We find groupings of mutually compatible memes in the brains of individuals. These are complexes of co-adapted memes that articulate and "cooperate" with each other, just as genes do to build the highly integrated and unified machines we call organisms. Religions and ideologies alike are convincing examples of meme complexes that codevelop in our brains and lead us to assemble in cooperative masses such as families, tribes or nations. I'll say more about this in a moment.

One of mankind's oldest memes is certainly the mastery of fire. It is not yet clear how long ago fire was first used by humans, as the question divides the scientific community[71]. Some authors - and this seems logical - believe that the very first fire used by human groups was taken from fires caused by lightning or volcanic eruptions. The ability to produce real fire is more recent. But whatever the dates, the most crucial thing is the transition from not using fire to using it, whether produced or not. Indeed, the mastery of fire is one of the characteristics that distinguishes the human lineage from the rest of the animal world. Indeed, the first *Homo erectus to* have the idea of using fire to improve the daily lives of his people was the inventor and creator of one of the very first memes. We know that its importance will be considerable for the rest of the human adventure. The fire meme is likely to have been quickly replicated across numerous communities of our distant ancestors. The success of this meme is explained by the progress it brought to the species. With fire, *erectus* could cook meat and digest it better, light the interior of the caves he used for shelter, and keep warm to avoid the terrible pneumopathies that used to decimate him. With fire, he learned to strengthen the points of his stakes to hunt better, and he also understood that flames kept predatory animals away and protected his children. The first hearths were probably the gathering points of small human groups, prototypes of our societies and political meetings. Finally, fire brought something that would radically differentiate man from all other animal species, enabling him to make considerable progress in his cerebral capacities: it gave him the ability to sleep peacefully. Thanks to fire, man can abstract himself from his environment, isolating himself and neglecting the outside

---

71. The earliest undisputed fireplaces date back some 400,000 years, and are more numerous around 200,000 BC. Certain fire production methods therefore probably date back to the Lower Paleolithic, even if direct archaeological evidence dates back no more than 9,000 years for friction methods (Guitarrero cave in Peru). Cf. PERLÈS (Catherine), *Préhistoire du feu*, Masson, 1977.

4. Genes and memes, the same battle

world for a time. This sensory break is essential to the development of the human psyche. The apes closest to man cannot enjoy the degree of security that fire has conferred on man; they are obliged to maintain a certain level of vigilance at all times; like many animals, they never sleep with more than one eye open. Humans are the only primates to sleep deeply, with long and repeated periods of REM sleep, the most restorative. During these periods, there is a collapse in muscle tone and a drop in the excitation of sensory sensors; these signals testify to the subject's disconnection from the surrounding world and a significant lowering of alertness. On the other hand, brain activity at the same time is intense, apparently linked to the processing and memorization of information acquired during wakefulness. With fire guaranteeing his safety, man cuts himself off from his environment to release his psychic functions, to dream, to imagine. In this way, he moves on to a new level of reflection, engaging in a never-ending process of action and feedback: freed from the external environment, he develops his intellectual faculties, which in turn free him even more from the contingencies of his environment, and so on[72].

It soon became clear to our *erectus* ancestors that the fire meme conferred considerable competitive advantages on those who possessed it. Humans who were the best at imitating and acquiring this meme soon became the most resistant. Their genetic line was endowed with greater brain power, since imitation is a difficult, energy-consuming exercise, and rather rare in the animal kingdom. The genes that gave them this ability, and the larger brains it required, spread throughout the gene pool. Everyone became better at imitating, increasing the pressure to keep enlarging the brain[73]. It was certainly at this point that a profound bifurcation took place in the evolutionary river

---

72. Cf. RUFFIÉ (Jacques), *De la biologie à la culture*, Flammarion, 1976.
73. Cf. BLACKMORE (Susan), *The Evolution of Meme Machines*, paper presented at the International Congress of Ontopsychology and Memetics, Milan, May 18-21, 2002.

of the human species. By imitating a new behavior or the skill of another hominid, the species would evolve differently, the biological organism gradually adapting to the thrust of mimetic desire and, consequently, that of memes. As soon as the first memes appeared, it became important to be able to acquire them, as they conferred a considerable advantage on those who welcomed them. This desire for appropriation through imitation is, according to René Girard, the foundation of the emergence of culture[74]. As more people became able to imitate, memes began to compete with each other to be copied and replicated from brain to brain. In the same human group, the individual who stood out from the others by a few striking features or an original discovery immediately became a model for the others, and thus the center of gravity towards which the whole group focused its desire. Memetic imitation works like a contagion, reaching people at their very core. Certain particularly useful functions, such as mastering fire or flint knapping, spread very quickly. But others appeared, more or less futile or fanciful, like decorating the body or painting the cave wall, or dancing under the moon. Like genes, memes make no distinction between right and wrong, useful or useless; what counts for them is to be replicated and to continue evolving.

By creating new forces of selective pressure, memes integrate humans into a limitless field of knowledge, traditions, myths and know-how. Man's biological and genetic development stabilizes when he reaches the *sapiens* stage; but the evolution of his brain never ceases to progress, opening up ever-new paths to culture. As Edgar Morin puts it, hominization is a kind of "definitive incompletion[75]", with the human brain continuing to enrich and develop, providing ever-new adaptations, while biological evolution tends to diminish. As adaptation is no longer genetic, but cultural, the evolution of humanity

---

74. Cf. GIRARD (René), *Les Origines de la culture*, Desclée de Brouwer, 2004.
75. *Morin (Edgar)*, Le Paradigme perdu. La Nature humaine, *Seuil, 1973*.

4. Genes and memes, the same battle

becomes the *history* of humanity, fragmenting it into a multitude of diverse cultures and human groups. Information, the fundamental fact of life, is no longer contained solely in chromosomes, but also in memes, conferring a new freedom on man, but also a responsibility in the face of the power he possesses; a power that will perhaps overtake him, too overwhelming for his human frailty.

Interlude IV

Humanity's first dispute

In the 1960s, Théodore Monod discovered a little book that made him choke with laughter. It was *Pourquoi j'ai mangé mon père*, by anthropologist Roy Lewis. The novel recounts the inventions and misadventures of Edouard, a hominin genius, opposed by his brother Vania, a prehistoric ecologist. The book was an instant worldwide success. I can't resist the temptation of transcribing this scene, humanity's first controversy on the risks of progress and the escalation of memes, when they hold the brains of men:

"The first argument I can remember between these brothers, so different in appearance and behavior, was about the fire. It was a cold day. I was crouched at a respectful distance from this squirming, red thing, brand new to us. It looked bruised but furiously ravenous, and I watched Father feed it with splendid but circumspect nonchalance. The women, all seated in a heap, were spooning each other and jabbering. My mother, as always, was a little out of the way. She was chewing the porridge for the weaned babies, and watching Father and his fire with an air of sombre meditation. Then, all of a sudden, Uncle Vanya appeared in our midst, a huge, menacing figure. He spoke in a voice from beyond the grave.

- There you are, Edouard!" he scolded. I should have guessed that sooner or later it would come to this. I guess I hoped there'd be a limit to your madness. Fool that I was: I only have to turn my back for a minute, to find you up to your neck in some new nonsense. And now this! Edward, listen to me. Haven't I warned you a thousand times, implored you, begged you, as your elder brother, to stop your calamitous course in time, to reflect, to mend your ways, and to change your life before it leads you and your whole family straight into irreversible disaster! This time, it's with tenfold insistence that I shout to you: Stop! Stop, Édouard, stop before it's too late, if there's even time, stop... [...] I've already told you a thousand times that, if you stay within reasonable limits, tools and punches don't really transgress nature. [...] You see, I'm ready to admit that it's legal to carve stones, because that's staying within the bounds of nature. Provided, however, that we don't become too dependent on it: stone cut for man, not man for stone cut! And that we don't want to refine them any more than necessary. I'm a liberal, Édouard, and my heart is on the left. So far, so good. But this, Édouard, this! That thing!" he says, pointing to the fire, "that's something else entirely, and no one knows where it will end. And it doesn't just concern you, Edouard, it concerns everyone! It concerns me! Because you could burn down the whole forest with a thing like that and what would become of me?

- Oh, Father, I don't think it will come to that!

- You really don't believe!" exclaimed the uncle. My word, Edouard, can we ask you if you've even mastered this... thing?

- Uh... well, more or less, probably. Yes, that's it, more or less. [...]

- How long have you been playing with fire?

- Oh, I discovered the trick over a month ago," says Father. Vanya, you don't realize, it's fascinating stuff. Absolutely fascinating. With prodigious possibilities! The heating alone would be a big step, but there are so many other things! I'm just beginning to make a serious study of it. It's mind-boggling. Take smoke: believe it or not, it suffocates flies and repels mosquitoes. Oh, of course, fire is a tricky thing to handle. Plus, it eats like an ogre. Rather nasty with it: at the slightest inattention, it stings you like the devil. But you see, it's really something new. It opens up endless perspectives and real...

A howl interrupted him. Uncle Vanya was dancing, hopping on one foot. I had noticed, with great interest, that for some time he had been standing on a glowing ember. Too excited by the fight to notice, he hadn't noticed the smell or the hiss. But now the ember had bitten right through the thick leather of his heel.

- Yah!" roared Uncle Vanya. "It bit me! Frog! You, Edouard, you fool, didn't I tell you? It'll eat you all, your stupid discovery! Ah, you want to dance on a live volcano! Edouard, I've had it with you! Your damn fire will extinguish you and your kind in no time, believe me! Yah! I'm going back up my tree, this time you've crossed the line, Edouard, and remember, the brontosaurus also crossed the line, where is it now? Farewell. *Back to the trees!*" he shouted as a rallying cry. Back to the trees[76]!

---

76. Lewis (Roy), *Pourquoi j'ai mangé mon père*, Actes Sud, 1990.

5. A meme machine

Scientists now know how to go back in time by studying the molecular clock inscribed in proteins and DNA. According to their research, we need to go back 5 million years to find an ancestor common to man and his closest cousin, the chimpanzee[77]. Australopithecines are descended from this common ancestor, and are found mainly in Africa. The first ancestor worthy of the name *Homo, Homo habilis, is* around 2,500,000 years old. Sometimes nicknamed "the tinkerer", he could build very basic stone implements. It was completely bipedal, but had difficulty running, and its head was much larger than that of its immediate ancestors, but much smaller than ours. He too would have developed in Africa; in the same basin, an improvement of the species appeared: *Homo erectus*. His cranium was larger, and he quickly discovered travel and set out to conquer the world, around 2 million years ago. The last species to appear 300,000 years ago, *Homo sapiens* has a skull and brain of almost identical volume to the one we have today. Yet its features are still simian, and it was only 100,000 years ago that we discovered individuals who so resemble us morphologically that you could pass them in the street without turning around.

---

77. We have to go back even further to find a branch that leads to our slightly more distant cousin, the gorilla. Going back another 13 million years, we find the fork in the road with a red-haired cousin, surprisingly similar to the human species: the orangutan.

The human brain grew steadily until *Homo sapiens sapiens*, and then its growth stopped. If we take a computer image, we could say that the *hardware* grew and reached a plateau, so the *software had to* change and become even more powerful.

There are many questions about the brain. Many have long remained unanswered; some still do. The first legitimate question is whether the human brain is composed of neuronal matter different from that of other animal species. Today, the answer is definitely no. Of course, the first thing that stands out is the incredible morphological diversity of brains in different living organisms. Diversity of size, shape and functional capacity. The smallest brains have a few hundred neurons, while others have several billion. The shapes are compact, elongated, bulging, with ganglia or extreme concentration, the inventory is particularly rich. However, all neurons, whatever the species, follow the same pattern[78]. They all have a cell body, dendrites that receive information from other neurons, and an extension of varying length: the axon. The axon transmits and distributes to other neurons or muscle fibers a message that synthesizes spatio-temporally all the information received. The interconnection of thousands or billions of neurons within a network forms the nervous system. In all species, synapses are the connectors between an axon and a dendrite, enabling communication to take place in chemical form. These chemical substances acting as mediators are relatively few in number, but they are broadly the same in all animal species. What makes the difference from one species to another is the nervous network. Specialists in comparative anatomy distinguish between three types: reactive, regulated and cognitive networks[79].

---

78. Cf. BUISSERET (Pierre), *Pas si bêtes ! Mille cerveaux, mille mondes*, Nathan, Coll. du Muséum national d'histoire naturelle, 1999.
79. Cf. BUISSERET (Pierre), "Évolution du cerveau et intelligence", in *L'intelligence*, ed. Jacques Lautrey and Jean-François Richard, Lavoisier, 2005.

Reactive networks are the basis of behaviors in which a stimulus always leads, via a reflex network, to the same motor reaction. They are characteristic of animals whose nervous systems do not exceed a few thousand or tens of thousands of neurons. The sea slug, for example, if touched, instantly triggers a cloud of ink to protect its escape. This very simple reactive network still exists in contemporary man, with the patellar, pupillary or blink reflexes, for example. As motor and sensory performance improves and becomes more sophisticated, these simple reflex networks are included, organized and modulated by other control networks: regulated networks. These networks make it possible to learn and memorize complex sequences of movements, provided they are successfully repeated many times. The sequence is always the same, reproduced in a stereotyped way. This is the case with certain animals that trigger hunting behavior by reacting to stereotyped shapes, whether animal or decoy. When you drive your car or ride your bike, your brain uses organized sequences of motor acts acquired through learning. This is made possible by the simple addition of control circuits to pre-existing nervous circuits.

Some animals are capable of practicing innovative behaviors: they conceptualize space, build tools or are able to anticipate the behavior of other individuals. Such behaviors call on a third type of network: the cognitive network, knowledge of which is still in its infancy. This network adds to and interacts with the previous two, implementing feedback loops on themselves. So, for example, they will be solicited by a stimulus, but the stimulus will be analyzed, and the information compared with that provided by other sensors or by memory. This results in the programming of a motor response, the outcome of which is anticipated and its relevance assessed. Once the action has been decided, the control networks are activated to orchestrate the entire process.

While the "raw material" of the brain is virtually the same in all animal species, the fact remains that human brains are capable of feats that surpass all other species on the planet. However, the skills we possess are not only superior to those of other animals, they are also *out of step with* them. We have brain functions that have developed over the course of evolution, but which don't seem to have been designed solely for the objective common to other species: survival.

Our brains have continued to grow in size; why this race towards ever greater volume? Our ancestor *Lucy*, the famous australopithecine discovered by Yves Coppens in Ethiopia, lived between 4 million and 2.5 million years ago. It was 1 m tall and had a brain not much bigger than that of a modern chimpanzee: 400 to 500 cm³. *Homo habilis*, *which* appeared later, knew how to cut stones and make rudimentary tools. His brain measured around 750 cm³. *Erectus*, discovered in the Kenyan fossil record, had a brain of almost 900 cm³; we know that he mastered fire and knew how to travel. The first *Homo sapiens* had a brain volume of around 1,100 cm³, gradually increasing to around 1,300 cm³. Bipedalism certainly favored brain development, for strictly mechanical reasons, in relation to the skeleton. In animals with a horizontal stature, the head is attached to the end of the spinal column by strong muscular straps, but this "leaning" position, which pushes the foramen magnum backwards, limits growth and mobility. In humans, on the other hand, the skull rests on the end of the spinal column, which has become vertical; it is therefore well balanced and can grow without difficulty in all its diameters. Standing was therefore probably a decisive factor in the increase in brain size. But that's where morphological evolution ended[80].

---

80. Biologist Jacques Ruffié notes that our upright posture is relatively recent in human development, so it has not been fully integrated into our genome. Bipedalism is certainly an exceptional achievement, given the small surface area of the human levitation polygon and our relatively high center of gravity. To compensate for these characteristics, we have developed highly sophisticated postural reflexes and balancing centers. On the other hand, we still have weaknesses linked to verticality, such as venous insufficiency in the lower limbs, often resulting in varicose veins, or fragility of the fourth and fifth lumbar vertebrae, which are put under heavy strain by standing upright. It should be noted that these types of pathologies are virtually non-existent in monkeys, and are, in their own way, unique to humans. Cf. Ruffié (Jacques), *op. cit.*

Indeed, over the last 100,000 years, human brain size has not changed: Cro-Magnon brain volume was the same as ours.

This massive, steady increase in brain size was very energy-intensive. As we know, the brain consumes around 20% of a human body's energy at rest. A smaller brain would be more energy-efficient, and nature doesn't waste energy without good reason. So why are we endowed with this enormous bulbous organ that is so metabolically greedy? What's more, the brain is a dangerously expensive organ. Neurons, and more specifically axons, are surrounded by a fatty sheath, myelin, which forms during foetal development and early childhood. This myelanization is a veritable turbo in the human brain: the sheath that covers certain parts of the axons leaves uncovered areas[81]. Myelin accelerates nerve conduction by enabling it to literally jump from one uncovered node to another. In a non-myelinated axon, the speed of propagation of action energy is 0.5 meters per second; in myelinated axons, the action potential travels at 120 m/s, or 400 km/h! This is what enables our brain to communicate with our big toe in a few hundredths of a second. But myelanization comes at a price: it drains the baby's resources considerably. What's more, human babies, with their disproportionately large heads for easy birth, are born prematurely compared to other animal species, especially monkeys. At birth, the human infant has a brain of around 385 cm^3, which triples in volume in the first two years of life. Whereas chimpanzees and orang-utangs bask in an intra-uterine life, our little humans are, at birth, defenseless against the influences of the outside world, malleable and incapable of autonomy. Whereas baby antelopes know how to run from birth, or baby turtles never know their parents, human babies are imperfectly formed and defenseless. Totally dependent with their big heads and puny bodies, they need a long period of maturation with their parents. In virtually all animal species, evolution has patiently protected the

---

81. These are Ranvier's knots.

baby's growth within the mother's body. In humans, this evolution has curiously reversed itself, endangering the process of genetic descent. On the other hand, another phenomenon has emerged, that of social life and the protection afforded by the human group. Human survival depended on the ability to live together. The origins of the family and civilization lie in the powerlessness of newborn humans. Females will seek out the male capable of protecting their offspring, gradually modifying their sexual strategies[82]. Men, for their part, will look for women with wide hips, capable of giving birth to children with minimum risk. The statuettes of the "fertility goddesses[83]", whose prehistoric remains can be found in a large number of sites, are all representations of females with wide hips and large buttocks, configured to sire children with larger brains.

The human brain is not only large in volume. It has three times as many nerve cells as the largest anthropomorph, the gorilla. If you carefully unfold the surface of the human brain, you'll see that it averages over 22,000 cm², two-thirds of which is buried deep in the sulci[84]. The gorilla's brain surface is only 5,500 cm². Moreover, the increase in brain volume has not been uniform: its masses are unevenly distributed. Thanks largely to advances in medical imaging, neurobiologists can now pinpoint the brain's functional zones. Our visual cortex, located at the very back of the brain, is relatively small, while our frontal cortex, located at the front and not directly mana-ging sensory information, is extremely developed. However, it is not

---

82. Unlike their close guenon cousins, female hominids lost estrus: they no longer went into "heat" at certain times of the year. They could experience sexual attraction at any time. This made them more attractive to males, who no longer had to wander around looking for sexual partners. The emergence of this physiological function enabled the construction of stable, protective families for human children. Cf. FISHER (Helen E.), *The Strategy of Sex*, Calmann-Lévy, 1982.
83. Cf. in particular the *Lespugue Venus* in the Musée de l'Homme in Paris.
84. Cf. RUFFIÉ (Jacques), *op. cit.*

yet clear what the frontal cortex does[85]. Other areas of the brain have undergone considerable reorganization over the course of evolution. These areas have evolved differently in humans than in other animal species. In most species, cries, songs and grunts originate in the mesencephalon, an area of the brain closely linked to emotions and responses to stimuli. In humans too, laughter and crying are produced by the midbrain. Human speech, on the other hand, is controlled by the cortex, and more specifically by the famous Broca's area, responsible for speech production, and Wernicke's area, dedicated to language comprehension.

Why has our brain evolved in this way? There are many theories, most of them inadequate and contradictory[86]. The first theories to address this question assert that tool manufacturing and technological innovations contributed to increasing the number of demands on the brain, which quickly had an impact on its volume. In the same vein, some hypotheses suggest that it was environmental pressure that drove the development of this organ. Humans needed to be sharper for hunting and survival in a hostile world. A larger brain meant greater skill, better hunting and longer survival. These theories are based on common-sense arguments, but why did we develop our brains so much? Many animals are very good at hunting, perhaps more so than humans, and have smaller brains. Why hasn't nature saved the disproportionate energy expenditure deployed by this human brain? Furthermore, these theories lead us into a vicious circle: did man need to eat more - especially meat - to feed his increasingly voracious brain?

---

85. Some people with severe lesions in this part of the brain function relatively well. We know the story, from 1848, of Phineas Gage, a railway worker whose frontal cortex was pierced through and through by a crowbar. His personality was of course considerably altered, but he could still walk, talk and appear normal to some degree.
86. Susan BLACKMORE provides a relatively exhaustive overview in *La Théorie des mèmes, op. cit.*

Or is it the other way round: did man hunt more and eat more meat, which would have had an effect on his brain, which, benefiting from the extra energy, would have expanded. Research on early hominids shows that they tended to gather and forage for food. Did they need an advanced brain to define conceptual maps of the spaces that could contain their sustenance? We've seen that other animals - such as bees - have much smaller brains than humans, yet manage to define highly precise cognitive maps.

Other theories focus on the social environment to explain the increase in human brain size. Some researchers believe that the first hominids to live in groups developed introspective abilities, which are essential to the smooth running of any society. Anticipating what my fellow human being will do if I perform a given action means putting myself in his or her shoes and imagining his or her reactions. Nicholas Humphrey, who developed this hypothesis, talks of *Homo psychologique*[87], i.e. the first human with self-awareness. Another version of social theory develops the hypothesis of a "Machiavellian intelligence", justified by the fact that social relations are particularly complex, requiring rapid and numerous adjustments, alliances, plots and ruses. The social theories put forward to explain the growth of the human brain are appealing, and to a large extent legitimate. But these theories overlook a fundamental stage: imitation.

Living in society means watching others, exchanging ideas, observing and often imitating. Imitation precedes and gives rise to the invention of society, with its codes and norms. Throughout his work, philosopher René Girard has developed the concept of *mimetic desire*[88]; this is always born of imitation, not only of the gestures or actions of another taken as a model, but also of one's own desire. Society was

---

87. HUMPHREY (Nicholas), *The Inner Eye: Social Intelligence in Evolution*, Oxford University Press, 2002.
88. Which today finds a neurophysiological foundation in the theory of "mirror neurons", which I'll discuss in Chapter 8.

born to channel this desire, which by its very nature tends to become antagonistic. Indeed, mimicry introduces rivalries and conflicts that society must structure and control[89]. However, if imitation leads to conflict, it also leads to culture, as it is the basis of all cultural transmission. Here we return to the heart of the meme question. The real turning point in human evolution, an important turning point with biological consequences for the size and organization of our brains, is that of imitation, capable of giving rise to a cultural replicator that is complementary to, but different in nature from, the gene: the meme.

You may say that imitation is found in nature in animal species other than humans. Certainly, primates, for example, are endowed with gestural and behavioral capacities that enable them to imitate. Numerous experiments demonstrate this, often in spectacular fashion. But we have already seen that human imitation has something special that makes it unique and distinctive in the animal kingdom: it can be replicated almost perfectly, because what is being copied are conceptually integrated instructions. This ability is the turning point in hominization; it is probably the moment when the ability to create concepts, to elaborate new mental models, to use imagination, emerges. This question is one of the great enigmas of cognitive science. American cognitive scientist and linguist Mark Turner argues that only human beings are capable of performing this highly advanced kind of conceptual integration[90], which would be the key to innovation, the springboard for a gigantic leap forward in evolution. According to him, conceptual integration is what enables human beings to develop new senses, understand disparate conceptual sets and compress them into a single mental space - the *blend* - that can be easily apprehended, manipulated and duplicated[91]. A process of conceptual integration

---

89. *Cf.* GIRARD (René), *Les Origines de la culture, op. cit.*
90. He calls this conceptual integration model: *double-scope* integration.
91. *Cf.* TURNER (Mark), *The Artful Mind: Cognitive Science and the Riddle of Human Creativity*, Oxford University Press, 2006.

means understanding that two stones picked up from a riverbed, if knocked together, will give rise to a new form endowed with specific, innovative functionalities: a tool. A tool is an object shaped to serve a purpose. The web spun by a spider is not, *strictly speaking,* a tool designed to catch insects, since this object is not artificial, but organic or more generally "natural", like a bird's nest or the dwellings of certain insect colonies. Similarly, the stick or pebble I pick up on the side of a path to use as an instant aid is not a tool, because it has not been intentionally created. The tool is therefore specifically human, as it does not derive from any organic function and is not subject to any biological organization. It is probably a sign of the transition from animal to human capacity for conceptual integration. Georges Bataille made no mistake: "The manufacture of tools and weapons was the starting point for the first reasoning processes that humanized the animal we were. Man, in shaping matter, knew how to adapt it to the end he had in mind. But this operation not only changed the stone [...]. Man changed himself: it was obviously the work that made him the human being, the reasonable animal that we are[92].

The earliest evidence of conceptual integration and imitation came in the form of stone tools, the earliest of which date back some 2,500,000 years. If you try to carve a stone into a suitable tool, you'll find that the art is particularly difficult. It may take a little time, trial and error and the loss of a few phalanges. But the leap forward you'll make in mastering this technique will only come through imitation of another, once you've integrated into your mental space that a common stone can become a tool, endowed with unprecedented, "unimaginable" functionalities. Having understood this mechanism, not only will you succeed faster, but you'll be able to pass on to someone else the secret and interest of your gestures, by breaking

---

92. Bataille (Georges), *Les Larmes d'Éros*, Pauvert, 2001.

them down into conceptually integrated units of information. This is certainly how the art of making stone tools spread through all primitive peoples. As new skills emerge, it becomes increasingly important to acquire and propagate them. The spiral of mimetic desire is on the move; it's inexorable, because the replication of memes depends on it. This art of imitation demands ever more sophisticated skills from your brain, which will be reproduced from generation to generation through the selection of the best imitator, since this one has an advantage over all the others in terms of survival and the guarantee of its genetic descendants.

It's quite likely that the emergence of language is linked to this simultaneous development of conceptual integration and imitation. Indeed, nothing beats the spoken word for transmitting instructions and propagating memes. But language is not a given in nature; it is an eminently human act. The Bible tells us that God created animals, but left it to Adam to name them[93]. Identifying a being or an object with a word is the first specifically human mission in history, a step that takes us beyond our animal nature.

Our closest evolutionary neighbors, chimpanzees and gorillas, can learn to communicate through language; they are capable of a vocabulary of around four hundred words, but cannot speak except by employing special tricks; indeed, they do not know how to use their tongue and pharynx to produce sounds comparable to ours. In truth, they do not have speech. They can use symbols to designate objects, they can understand the association of certain symbols with words, but they cannot form sentences, let alone understand the rudiments of grammar or syntax. Our primate friends have to suffer to carry out these kinds of experiments; their learning is necessarily long, laborious and built on a succession of rewards and punishments. In

---

93. Gn II, 19.

humans, language is almost a matter of instinct[94]; all humans can speak, effortlessly; they all know how to form roughly grammatically correct sentences, regardless of their intelligence or education; all the languages spoken on our planet can be learned, and have more or less the same types of difficulties; there is no such thing as a "primitive" language, less evolved than another. How did human beings acquire this unique skill? No one knows for sure; some think it came about all of a sudden, as a kind of "systemic catastrophe[95]" in the course of evolution. Renowned linguist Noam Chomsky believes that our linguistic structures are innate, and that languages share a common "deep structure"[96]. Anthropologist Stephen Jay Gould shares Chomsky's view that the emergence of language was not the result of an evolutionary process, but the side-effect of another phenomenon, such as the increase in brain size[97]. Other scientists, such as Pinker, believe that language is the result of a process of natural selection, and that it developed according to a classic Darwinian model. Whatever these differences of opinion may be, they do not provide any answers as to the nature of the selective advantage conferred by mastery of language. What's more, it's impossible to precisely date the appearance of language, so the mystery remains. The fossil record is, of course, non-existent, and paleontological research on the subject is contradictory. Could *Homo habilis* speak? We can't say for sure. We can see from the traces left on his first carved stones that he must have been right-handed. However, lateralization goes hand in hand with the development of the area dedicated to language, located in the left hemisphere of the brain. But this observation is not proof enough. Speaking requires not only a particular cerebral organization, but

---

94. Cf. PINKER (Steven), *The Language Instinct*, Odile Jacob, 1999.
95. DEACON (Terence W.), *The Symbolic Species. The Co-Evolution of Language and the Brain*, New York, W. W. Norton & Cy, 1997.
96. Cf. CHOMSKY (Noam), *Le Langage et la Pensée*, Payot, 1990.
97. *Cf.* GOULD (Stephen Jay), *The Structure of Evolutionary Theory, op. cit.*

also an adapted physiological one: we need to be able to control our breathing, which implies a modification of the diaphragm and chest muscles; the varied sounds of language are only clearly produced when the larynx is lower than that of our primate cousins. What's more, the shape of the base of the skull also affects the range of possible sounds. Under these conditions, *Homo sapiens* is much better equipped to speak than his ancestor *erectus*. Modern language would therefore probably only have appeared 100,000 years ago, at the earliest. All these clues, however, leave us with no definitive hypothesis. We can only speculate that *Lucy* couldn't speak, and that *erectus* conversations around the fire must have been particularly limited.

Pro- or anti-Darwinian explanations don't really help us to understand the nature of the emergence of language. The reason for this impasse probably lies in the exclusively genetic perspective adopted by most theories on the subject. But it was geneticist (and linguist) Luca Cavalli-Sforza who put us on the right track. According to him, "language is *both a* genetic and a cultural innovation", and he goes on to describe, without ever mentioning the word, the theory of memes: "Culture is similar to genetic inheritance insofar as both accumulate very useful information from generation to generation. The genome duplicates itself through the duplication of DNA; cultural information duplicates itself by passing from the nerve cells of one individual's brain to another[98]." The relationship between language and culture is obviously very tenuous: "In man, language is the basis of culture[99]", asserts Cavalli-Sforza, so the path leading to the hypothesis that language emerged to propagate memes is relatively straightforward. Susan Blackmore resolutely follows this path: "It is memetic selection, along with genetic selection, that is at work in creating language[100]."

---

98. Cavalli-Sforza (Luca), *Gènes, peuples & langues*, Odile Jacob, 1996 (emphasis added).
99. *Ibid.*
100. Blackmore (Susan), *Meme Theory, op. cit.*

According to the renowned neurologist John C. Eccles, winner of the Nobel Prize for Medicine, language areas are formed in the human brain before birth, so their construction at this stage obeys a process that is genetically coded. This is why the development of language regions in this way enables us to learn all languages, whatever they may be. He also believes that the deep structure of grammar, as described by Chomsky, is similar to the micro-organization of the brain's linguistic areas. The child is thus born with knowledge of the deep structure of language, because he or she is genetically equipped with it from before birth[101].

At birth, the genetic structure of language develops through memetic processes. Since memes are transmitted by imitation, language is obviously a very powerful means of increasing the efficiency not only of the imitation process, but also of the replication process. As we have seen, the hallmark of human imitation is the ability to reproduce "instructions". The transmission of these instructions is greatly facilitated if we can break down a gesture, for example, into a sequence of well-defined, "codified" steps. In genetics, replication is facilitated and guaranteed with almost absolute reliability because there is a digital code. I've already mentioned this in a previous chapter. In the same vein, language can be seen as the digitization of sounds into words. Language in fact consists of a set of small sounds that have no meaning in themselves, *phonemes*, but which, combined together, form words that signify things[102]. These words are coded in a way that is strong enough to be precisely duplicated. Language would thus have emerged by selecting and codifying in the form of clearly identified words,

101. *Cf.* Eccles (John C.), *Evolution of the Brain and the Creation of Consciousness*, Flammarion, 1994.
102. Of the thousands of languages spoken on the planet, some contain only a variety of nineteen phonemes. The most phoneme-rich language has no more than seventy-five. Yet these numbers are more than enough to produce an almost infinite number of different words.

what at first, in the days of the "primitive soup", was no more than grunts or borborygms. Imagine a prehistoric hunter's meal: gathered around the fire, they enjoy their well-deserved dinner after a long day's stalking. Filled with satisfaction, they emit vocal sounds to express their pleasure. These sounds, when repeated, become words for objects. The word "mammoth" - or its prehistoric equivalent - for example, could have been born when one of the men in the group, licking his lips, let out a grunt of sonorous satisfaction, which intrigued his fellows. The word must have been repeated, then associated with images, sounds, smells and perhaps hunting situations. This is how the initial vocabulary developed, with its strong survival value[103]. Language thus made a considerable leap forward in the propagation of memes. Not only did it make it possible to transmit information more precisely, it also offered high-fidelity duplication. What's more, language considerably increased the possibility of memorizing gestures, customs, stories and rituals, which gradually invaded the mental space of the first humans gifted with speech. Language thus consists in the emergence of a mechanism for digitizing words; grammar, for its part, being the instrument that multiplies the possibilities of encoding words. It is grammar that enables us, with a relatively limited number of words, not only to describe the riches of the world, but also to evoke the most abstract ideas, inflect our thoughts, finely nuance our proposals, write instructions or tragedies.

The memetic influence on the emergence of language is a hypothesis. This theory is strengthened when we correlate it with the idea we developed earlier of the presence of digital information at the very heart of life. Since language is what will enable human culture to develop across the entire planet, it seems logical to consider that this evolution cannot be carried out in any other way than by finding a way to digitize information in general and memes in particular. We shall see that this process is still underway, and that it is not about to stop.

---

103. *Cf.* Margulis (Lynn), *The Bacterial Universe, op. cit.*

Interlude V

Heritage

"I looked at the mother, that old peasant woman with her peaceful, hard face and tight lips, that face turned into a mask of stone. And I recognized the sons' faces. This mask had been used to imprint theirs. This body had been used to imprint these bodies, these fine specimens of men. And now it lay broken, but like a gangue from which the fruit has been removed. In their turn, sons and daughters, from their flesh, would print little men. We wouldn't die on the farm. The mother is dead, long live the mother!

Painful, yes, but so simple, this image of the lineage, abandoning one by one, on its way, its beautiful white-haired remains, walking towards I don't know what truth, through its metamorphoses.

That's why, that same evening, the death bell in the little country village seemed to me to be charged, not with despair, but with a discreet, tender joy. This bell, which celebrated funerals and baptisms with its voice, was once again announcing the passage from one gene-ration to the next. And there was nothing but peace in hearing her sing of the betrothal of a poor old woman to the earth.

What was passed on from generation to generation, with the slow progress of a growing tree, was not only life but also consciousness.

What a mysterious ascent! From molten lava, from star paste, from a living cell miraculously germinated, we have risen, little by little, to write cantatas and weigh Milky Way.

The mother had not only passed on life: she had taught her sons a language, entrusting them with the baggage so slowly accumulated over the centuries, the spiritual heritage she herself had received as a deposit, that small batch of traditions, concepts and myths that makes all the difference between Newton or Shakespeare and the cave-dwelling brute[104]."

104. SAINT-EXUPÉRY (Antoine de), *Terre des Hommes*, Gallimard, 1939.

6. Propagation

Like genes, memes are selected on the basis of the presence and richness of other memes in the same memetic pool, i.e. the complex of memes that coexist in the human brain. We find ourselves in a situation very similar to that of genes, which form coherent, cooperative groups designed to perform a function or achieve a goal: this is how the highly sophisticated organisms of most living beings are formed. The memes that best resist selection are those that encounter other complementary memes in the brain, with which they can implement a form of "cooperation". A memetic pool is then formed, made up of mutually compatible memes; the resulting gradual enrichment increasingly ensures its chances of replication and lasting propagation. This is where the notion of conceptual integration, to which I referred earlier, needs to be enriched to take man one step further than his previous evolutionary stage. We know that conceptual integration gives human beings the ability to create new meanings, new concepts and new mental models. It was thanks to conceptual integration that man invented the first tools and the rudiments of language. But as memetics evolves, meanings, concepts and models diversify, enrich and accumulate. How then can we apprehend and manipulate heterogeneous meanings, and link them together in dynamic conceptual networks? How can memory conjure them up, how can imagination bring them to life?

The evolutionary leap lies in the ability to manipulate complex sets of conceptual networks, bringing about what Mark Turner calls the *blend*[105], i.e. integrating heterogeneous and complex conceptual networks into a single concept - a condensation of memes or information. Here's an example to clarify the fundamental question that distinguishes man from every other species on the planet. If you have the opportunity to go for a walk to Lascaux, contemplating the cave paintings you'll discover there will assure you of one unshakeable certainty: these drawings were made by men. You certainly won't even ask yourself the question, because you intuitively know that image-based representation is specifically human in nature. This is not just a difference of degree between man and other animal species, but a difference of essence: there are no further refinements to be added and no transitions to be expected in such an evolution. Why are these paintings so specifically human? Because they are apparently *useless*. They do not seek to transform the surrounding world, nor the state of the organism. They have no biological purpose.

Images require a particularly complex process of conceptual integration, involving the construction of a likeness that is not a reproduction of an original, or a simulation, but a *representation*. In other words, you have to be able to suggest, by means of a few "representative" features, an economical selection of signs: by omission, simplification, exaggeration, distortion, stylization. The only thing that counts is the intention, which must be recognizable. Here again, the image is a "digitization" of reality: it represents it in the form of simple signs and graphic codes that can be easily reproduced and duplicated. But even more than this, the image detaches itself from the object, acquiring its independence and, by interposing itself with reality, making its presence freely available. This availability is then activated by a motor that calls up the memory and represents it; this motor is the

---

105. Cf. TURNER (Mark), *op. cit.*

one by which man conquers a new territory: that of the imagination. At Lascaux, writes Georges Bataille, "youthful humanity, for the first time, measured the extent of its richness [...], that is, the power it had to attain the unhoped-for, the *marvelous*[106]." This opens up an infinite field of variations, an *art form*, a field of possibilities, that man can realize according to his own choice. The most characteristic feature of hominization is certainly the development of this capacity for imagination. If we place a chimpanzee and a human in the same place, we will observe that both chimpanzees and humans perceive more or less the same sensory information. But if the chimpanzee knows, the human knows that he knows. He is self-aware, and thus aware of the space around him and the passage of time. Like all animals, a monkey almost always lives in the present, with little regard for the past or the future. They act in the moment, as circumstances dictate. At best, they can develop a very short-term strategy. Man, on the other hand, projects himself into the future using his imagination, and analyzes his present in the light of past experience. In this way, he can envisage multiple eventualities, foresee them and find solutions before being forced to by necessity. This self-awareness and ability to project oneself into the future are certainly at the origin of the idea of death. Russian biologist and geneticist Theodosius Dobzhansky, one of the most eminent protagonists of evolutionary theory, describes this emergence particularly well: "Self-awareness is indeed the most fundamental characteristic of the human species. It represents a novelty, for the species from which humanity descended had only rudimentary self-awareness, or even none at all. And yet, self-awareness brings with it sinister companions: fear, anxiety, awareness of death. Thus, a being who knows he will die one day was born of ancestors who did not know it[107]." Animals don't

---

106. Bataille (Georges), *Lascaux ou la Naissance de l'art*, Geneva, Albert Skira, 1980.
107. Dobzhansky (Theodosius), *Biology of Ultimate Concern*, New York American Library, 1967.

seem to know death, nor can they foresee it or be aware of it. When a young chimpanzee dies, the mother holds it in her arms for a while, then treats it as mere waste. No animal buries its dead, and very few continue to pay attention to them. Awareness of death and the rites attached to it are specifically human, and are lost in the mists of time, through a set of representations and *beliefs*.

Religion, or to put it more accurately, "the experience of the sacred[108]", is probably one of mankind's earliest co-adapted meme complexes. As soon as man was sufficiently equipped biologically to be able to "imagine", i.e. when he was able to conceptually integrate information in order to conjure up an image or an idea[109], his mind immediately led him to defy the appearance of his finitude and to move beyond the visible towards a restless questioning of the reality around him. We have no archaeological evidence of the anxieties of early man, but we can imagine them from the accounts brought back by anthropologists from their travels in so-called primitive societies. In 1929, one of the most famous explorers, Knud Rasmussen, brought back the testimony of the Aua shaman[110] from his expedition to the Thule lands. "*Fear* is omnipresent, haunting", he says. It is the focus of all attention and behavior. Fear of bad weather, fear of not having food, fear of hunger, fear of the moon, fear of the cold, fear of illness, fear of suffering, fear of death, fear of the dead. The first men certainly knew that misfortune could strike at any moment, that the evening meal was not assured or that they could be devoured at any moment by a ferocious beast. No one can live in apprehension of the chaos of things. Man needs to find a powerful, rich and reassuring meaning in the reality that surrounds him. To achieve this, he will

---

108. ELIADE (Mircea), *La Nostalgie des origines*, Gallimard, 1971.
109. Evolutionary psychologists refer to this as "inference" and "decoupling". Cf. BOYER (Pascal), *Et l'homme créa les dieux*, Robert Laffont, 2001.
110. *Cf.* RASMUSSEN (Knud), *Across Arctic America: Narrative of the Fifth Thule Expedition (1929)*, University of Alaska, 1999.

delve into his memory and make the prodigious effort, which will make him *human*, of conceptually integrating the fact that if he is here, it's because others have been here before him. And that despite the dangers, misfortunes and death they too faced, they survived and passed on life. Their descendants have received from them a set of prescriptions, instructions and prohibitions - memes - such that, if we observe them exactly, we can, like them, avoid succumbing and ensure the perpetuity of the group. Replicating ancestral memes and strictly imitating them then becomes a means of survival in a world of fear. You'll know which animals are easy to hunt and you won't starve; you'll know which plants heal and you'll be cured; tradition offers a response to every danger, and thus becomes almost sacred. The strict observance of rules that have proved their worth in ancestral times is a guarantee of survival for the human group[111]. If they are violated, order is disrupted and the whole of human life becomes impossible. A new conceptual space emerges: the ancestors who transmitted the memes take on the status of invisible, supernatural forces, with whom a pact has been made; anyone who breaks this pact endangers their own existence and that of the entire social group. The "sacred" then becomes the form of imitation of paradigmatic models revealed by supernatural Beings, which gives meaning to life. As man cannot live in chaos, the imitation of transhuman models seems an appropriate response, and thus forms one of the first characteristics of "religious" life[112]. The religious quest will then be that of interpreting "messages" or "words" from ancestors, heroes or gods, which must be deciphered to guide man's present life. For all these memes - ways of living, rules, customs - all that these men know, it is beings of another nature than themselves who have established or instituted them, and who have

---

111. *Cf.* Lévy-Bruhl (Lucien), *Le Surnaturel et la nature dans la mentalité primitive*, PUF, 1963.
112. Cf. Eliade (Mircea), *op. cit.*

transmitted them to them. This is how *rituals* appear, crystallizing a certain number of beliefs and behaviors through repetition; they regulate work and days, major obligations and minor gestures. As Marcel Gauchet points out in his *Disenchantment of the World*: "The entire framework into which the practice of the living-present flows stems from a founding past that rites constantly reactivate as an inexhaustible source and reaffirm in their sacred otherness[113]." Here we see the prodigious power of the memetic machine: it demands replication, it passes from brain to brain, it guides the smallest details of human life, it forges the nascent social bond within the framework of the taboo. From then on, the sacred can emancipate itself and cover the whole of man's environment: his ancestors, the animals he hunts, fears or feeds, nature in all its forms: trees, plants, stars, planets, winds, seas, lightning, volcanoes - everything that is real to man takes on sacred value. Obeying them brings the supreme values of rest and tranquility. Obedience is both the fear of punishment *and* a form of intellectual relaxation in the face of the dangers and questions of reality that arise every day. Effort fatigue and the need for ecstasy, reproduced by memetic imitation, reinforce religious sentiment everywhere. Its scrupulous replication avoids the effort of thinking and the pangs of anguish, liberating people and relieving them when they feel lost and call out for help. A sense of the sacred brings inner peace, hope and confidence. In neurobiological terms, it stimulates our brain's reward system, which is triggered by the activation of neuromodulators such as dopamine or opiates. It's only a short step from there to thinking that the "opium of the people" has a neuronal truth[114].

In his study of taboos, Freud describes them as a series of limitations, rational or not, understandable or not, to which men submit, unaware of the reasons for this or that prohibition; the idea does not

---

113. GAUCHET (Marcel), *Le Désenchantement du monde*, Gallimard, 1985.
114. Cf. CHANGEUX (Jean-Pierre), *L'Homme de vérité*, Odile Jacob, 2004.

even occur to them to seek them out: "They submit to them as to natural things and are convinced that a violation would automatically call down upon them the most rigorous punishment[115]". He observes that these prohibitions are maintained from generation to generation and transmitted by paternal or social authority. A few pages later, Freud introduces the idea of *contagion*. He observes that the man who breaks the taboo becomes taboo himself, because "he is really *contagious*, insofar as his example encourages imitation, and that is why he himself must be avoided[116]". A behavior would then be transmitted like an epidemic, but using - like any meme - the vector of imitation. Deepening his reflection, Freud notes that taboos are transmitted in part by tradition, but that some of them have become "an *organic* part of the psychic life of subsequent generations[117]". He adds that it is impossible to distinguish whether these prohibitions or directives are "innate ideas", echoing an old formula used by Descartes, or whether they are formed by education. Bergson describes these obligations as a "categorical imperative", *instinctive* in nature[118].

The inventor of psychoanalysis was unaware of memetic theory and its analogy with genetics. Nevertheless, the question is clearly posed: can cultural information be transmitted hereditarily, and thus acquire a certain form of innateness? Is it subject to Darwinian evolution? Can we speak of cultural evolution as we do of genetic evolution? The answers to these questions are still highly uncertain and controversial. It's true that this field of study lies at the confluence of a huge variety of biological and human scientific disciplines: genetics, population ecology, human paleontology, archaeology, prehistory, ethology, neurophysiology, psychology, linguistics, cognitive science, anthropology, sociology, economics and philosophy. To complicate matters,

---

115. FREUD (Sigmund), *Totem and Taboo (1913)*, Payot, 1947.
116. *Ibid.*
117. *Ibid.*
118. *Cf.* BERGSON (Henri), *Les Deux Sources de la morale et de la religion*, PUF, 1932.

this theme has particularly vivid ideological implications, rekindling old demons such as the debate on the relationship between race and culture, conveying powerful affects that sometimes impede lucid reflection. The fundamental question is to what extent cultural traits - memes - are the result of development and evolution, independent of genetics. In other words, the question boils down to whether memes lead their lives freely, or whether they are "kept on a leash[119]" by genetics.

In 2003, geneticists succeeded in deciphering the entire human genome by sequencing the thirty thousand or so genes present in DNA. This is a prodigious achievement, but it not only answers questions long left unanswered by biology, it also opens the way to new questions concerning the study of the human being in his or her development, not only as an individual, but also culturally. How can we explain, with just thirty thousand genes, the uniqueness of individuals and their extraordinary cultural diversity? How can we explain the complexity of the billions of interconnected neurons in the human brain, compared with the small number of genes that govern their construction[120]? Ever since we learned more about genetics, the mystery of the relationship between genes and culture has been deepening. The human genome differs from that of the chimpanzee by less than 2%, and it's still not clear what role this famous 2% plays. The genes involved in our brain development are nothing special compared to those of primates. In fact, these genes are expressed outside the brain and are very similar to those of other species. The "brain gene" simply doesn't exist. You might say, "Yes, but humans can talk, whereas monkeys can't!" I can see that you've read

---

119. The formula "Genes keep culture on a leash" is put forward by Edward O. WILSON in *L'Humaine Nature. Essai de sociobiologie*, Stock, 1979.
120. Cf. ORIGGI (Gloria), "Gènes et culture", in *Dictionnaire du corps*, Michela Marzano (dir.), PUF, 2007.

the previous chapter, but here again, geneticists are relatively formal: the "language gene" doesn't exist either.

Over the last thirty years or so, numerous models have emerged to answer the questions we ask ourselves. In 1975, Edward O. Wilson, a professor of zoology at Harvard University, published a book that caused quite a stir: *Sociobiology, The New Synthesis*[121]. Sociobiology closely links biology and culture. The central hypothesis is that animal and human social behavior has been and continues to be shaped by natural selection. According to this theory, behavior that *a priori* appears to be the product of moral or cultural motivation is in reality the expression of natural predispositions, selected according to the adaptive advantages they confer, in the strictest Darwinian sense. In other words, it's genes that keep culture on a tight leash.

Of course, this theory has not gone unchallenged. Anthropologists point out that there is what they call a "psychic unity of the human species". This means that the psychological differences between individuals or populations, particularly with regard to their cognitive capacities, are too small and too dispersed to explain the immense diversity of human cultures. Biologists, on the other hand, point out that the possibilities of variation in gene expression as a function of environment are too small in relation to the amplitude and richness of cultural differences. Evolutionary psychologists counter Wilson's theory with an argument that most sociobiologists now accept: genes have no effect on culture, but on mental mechanisms. It is the latter that have been selected during evolution, not socio-cultural behaviours[122]. It would be beyond the scope of this book to make an exhaustive inventory of theories, their arguments and counter-arguments; they are numerous and often extremely contradictory.

---

121. French translation: *La Sociobiologie*, Éditions du Rocher, 1987.
122. *Cf.* BARKOW (Jerome H.), Cosmides (Leda) & Tooby (John), *The Adapted Mind: Evolutionary Psychology and the Generation of Culture*, Oxford University Press, 1992.

The hypothesis that makes the most sense to me is that of a joint evolution between genes and the units of cultural information that are memes. In some cases, it's the genes that predominate - "holding the leash", to use Wilson's expression. In other cases, it's the memes - the cultural units - that take over. In all cases, the evolution of the two replicators is *joint*; it is consubstantial with every human being. This hypothesis has now become commonplace; it is developed mainly by the biological anthropologist Robert Aunger; I will return to his conclusions in the next chapter. The example of the evolution of brain size I mentioned earlier is a good illustration of this joint evolution between memetic and genetic pressure. Clearly, the brain could not have developed without genetic modifications, but it is equally clear that these transformations did not necessarily respond to a strictly genetic interest. In fact, it has been observed that the development of the brain, in this respect, ran rather counter to the interests of the survival of the species. In this case, memetic pressure was stronger.

Before going into this theoretical digression on the relationship between culture and genes, we were talking about religion. Here too, interesting examples show the dependence or independence of genes on memes. Most religions have their origins in social groups, often restricted to kin. Genetic homogeneity, naturally conferred by heredity between relatives, goes hand in hand with relative memetic homogeneity. Traditions, modes of dress or diet, language, customs and lifestyles in general are characteristic of a well-identified popu-lation type, usually a tribe. It was in this type of soil that religions - which are, let's not forget, a complex of co-adapted memes - took root. The ancient Hebrews are typical of the tribal groupings that were common at the time. Their tribes were homogeneous, made up of individuals descended from a few well-identified families. The outward signs of recognition of such tribes were clearly established by their way of life and, above all, by their belief in a God, in the rites attached to him, and in a solidly codified memetic and genetic

92

transmission[123]. As a result, the ancient Hebrews made little effort to convert other populations, as this would have made no sense from the point of view of the genetic *and* memetic homogeneity of their group. This concept was not particularly exclusive to the Hebrews; most peoples around the world practiced it.

Around 2,000 years ago, Jesus of Nazareth, a Jew, entered history. Like all other Jews of his time, he believed that God was the God of his genetic ancestors, Abraham and Jacob. Jesus preached only to Jews[124], to whom he was attached by god and genes. When he was crucified, his disciples - Jews - continued to carry his message to other Jews, trying to persuade them that Jesus was the Messiah and that he was seated on the throne of King David, to whom God had promised to "seat a descendant of his blood[125]" to protect his people. The disciples courageously continued to spread the word, despite fierce resistance. Their messages were always addressed to other Jews, whom they tried to convince against all odds. There was no question of speaking to anyone but Jews. This extraordinarily powerful homogeneity between memes and genes, to use our terminology, would shatter a few years after Jesus' death, with the appearance of an immense but ambiguous figure who would fundamentally mark the history of Christianity: Saul of Tarsus, known to posterity as Paul. Saul was a Jew from Tarsus, capital of the Roman province of Cilicia, and his father had made him a Roman citizen. A zealot of tradition, he could not stand the disorders caused by the disciples of Jesus. With passion and passion, he pursued them, persecuted them and, like Stephen, had them stoned to death by the hostile crowd. Recognized for his effectiveness in fighting what

---

123. In the Old Testament, God's covenant with Abraham is expressed as follows: "I will make you exceedingly fruitful... I will establish my covenant between me and you, and your seed after you, from generation to generation, an everlasting covenant, to be your God and the God of your seed after you." Gen XVII, 7.
124. The Greeks he also addressed, present in Galilee, were relatively few in his audience.
125. Ac, II, 30.

were not yet called Christians, he was sent to Damascus to quell a rebellion. The story goes that, on the way, he had a vision of Jesus, which turned his life upside down. Instantly, Saul called himself Paul, declared himself an apostle and pledged to carry "the Good News" by converting as many Jews as possible to the ideas of Jesus, to spread the new meme as widely as possible, but always within the same gene pool. This was no easy task, for Paul's troubled past had branded him with suspicion, and the community of Jesus' disciples took a dim view of the arrival of this troublesome figure who was reinterpreting the ideas of a Jesus he had never known. Paul, though tireless in his efforts and travels, struggled in his mission to spread the Gospel among the Jewish communities. Finally, exasperated, he decided that since the Jews wouldn't listen to him, he would go and talk to the others, the pagans[126]: Greeks, Romans, Anatolians, Sicilians or Spaniards. This event took place precisely in the synagogue of Antioch; at that moment and in that place, memes separated from genes and took on their autonomy. The tremendous rise of the Christian religion and its worldwide spread can be traced back to this singular moment. As memeticist Howard Bloom writes: "When Paul separated genes and gods, he unleashed a force that would unite super-organisms on a scale unprecedented in the world. He enabled the meme to become the most powerful form of replicator[127]."

How can memes propagate so powerfully? How do they jump from one brain to another? How are they replicated and sustained? To formulate answers to these questions, we need to enter the research laboratories of the cognitive sciences and delve into the mysteries of the brain, particularly those of memory. Animals only store in their

---

126. Acts, XIII, 45-46: "The word of God was to be proclaimed to you first. Since you reject it and do not consider yourselves worthy of eternal life, well then, we turn to the Gentiles... Thus the word of the Lord spread throughout the whole region."
127. BLOOM (Howard), *The Lucifer Principle*, Le Jardin des livres, 2001.

memory what they have acquired through their senses. Humans, on the other hand, can recall a past they have no direct personal experience of. This is how we acquire much of our knowledge and cultural baggage. But whether it's a legend handed down from generation to generation, a taboo or a social prohibition, a tool or a way of avoiding danger, all this information is an external trace that must pass into the individual's memory. An internal representation must be formed in the neural networks of each individual. External information must resonate with thought patterns already present in the brain. This is how memes draw their energy to spread ever more widely.

Interlude VI

Compagnie du Mont-Pèlerin

How has the liberalism meme taken hold in today's world? What paths did it take to become the substantial force of globalization? To understand the origins of this extraordinary dynamic, we need to go back to 1944 and Friedrich August von Hayek's seminal book, *The Road to Serfdom*[128]. This book is a passionate attack on state restrictions on the free functioning of market mechanisms. But this message did not resonate with the conceptual schemes of the minds of the time; it was simply not heard; post-war Europe was developing the foundations of social democratic states everywhere. So, in 1947, Von Hayek gathered the followers of his ideas in a small Swiss resort called Mont-Pèlerin. The participants were, or were to become, eminent figures such as Milton Friedman, Walter Lippman, Karl Popper, Ludwig von Mises and Maurice Allais. At the end of this meeting, the *Compagnie du Mont-Pèlerin* was founded, a well-structured organization to promote the ideas that nobody yet called *neoliberal*. The company set itself several objectives. The first of these was to fight Keynesianism and the post-war models of social solidarity head-on. Another objective requires time and resources: to lay the foundations for the future of

---

128. Cf. HAYEK (Friedrich August von), *The Road to Serfdom*, PUF, 1993.

pure capitalism, free of all rules and regulations, and the advent of a market economy in its most competitive form. At the time, the Compagnie du Mont-Pèlerin's approach went against the grain of all prevailing thinking. These ideas were all the more peculiar given that the economy was about to enter a rather long phase of growth; it was experiencing its golden age and entering its "Trente Glorieuses". The neoliberal current therefore appeared to have little credibility in its warnings and offensives against the State. This led to a long period in the wilderness, until 1974. During this period, he maintained, against all odds, the orthodoxy of his ideas and his determination to disseminate them. The first elements of an information network that would become global a few years later were formed. The first *think tanks were* created, and the Compagnie du Mont-Pèlerin continued its meetings and numerous publications (it later organized the Davos Economic Forum). The neoliberal network relied on the media - especially the Anglo-Saxon media - which grew in importance during this period.

In the mid-1970s, the oil crisis dealt the first blow to Keynesianism; the landscape of the welfare state was darkened by the spectres of mass unemployment and inflation. All the developed countries went into recession, and neoliberal ideas began to gain ground and, buoyed by the burgeoning wave of hyperinformation, began their memetic spread throughout the world.

Margaret Thatcher's Britain was a pioneering field of neoliberalism. Ronald Reagan's United States made use of neoliberal networks, recruiting Milton Friedman into the heart of the American presidency. In Europe, despite the reluctance of traditionally social-democratic countries and the electoral victories of left-wing parties in the 1980s, neoliberalism continued to develop. In France, Mitterrand's socialist project held out for less than two years, before radically changing policy in March 1983, taking the country in a direction very close to neoliberal orthodoxy. In Spain, Felipe Gonzalez's Socialist government put monetarism in the driving seat, favored financial capitalism, embarked on privatizations and remained calm in the face of record unemployment of 20% of the working population. In Australia, New Zealand and Latin America, the same neoliberal scheme is being triumphantly implemented, as in most OECD countries. In the 1990s, neoliberalism found a second wind, coming from the countries of Eastern Europe. When the Berlin Wall fell in 1989, the new architects of post-communist economies in Eastern Europe became zealous disciples of the theories of von Hayek and Friedman. The neoliberal tidal wave also reached Asia. Both the Indian and Chinese economies were subjected to vast structural adjustment plans.

This memetic current therefore has a truly global dimension, the likes of which capitalism has never produced before. Neoliberalism has developed absolutely throughout the world by two means: a strong symbolic discourse and a network of prescribers particularly powerful in replicating memes. The neoliberal discourse relies on a lexicon of new terms propagated *ad libitum* throughout the world: globalization, governance, flexibility, multiculturalism, identity, post-modernism, modernization and so on. This new discourse, this form of "pensée unique", is not only promoted by neo-liberal supporters, but also by the vast majority of what are known as "intellectuals": academics, writers, researchers, journalists; and by a great many personalities, even ordinary citizens, traditionally situated on the left of the political spectrum. The cloud of words making up the memetic complex of modern liberal thought is thus literally planetarized, multiplied to epidemic proportions worldwide by international media feedback. It circulates around the world through the channels of a highly organized network whose nodes are apparently neutral bodies: major international organizations such as the World Bank, the European Commission and the OECD. It relies on a meticulously organized network of *think tanks*. The discourse produced is then the work of a new breed of intellectual prescribers: the *experts*, who produce highly technical, scientific and even mathematical reports containing the analyses and recommendations that feed the brains of politicians and corporate decision-makers. All the world's major media serve as relays, with editorial writers and columnists eager to propagate the new language, a symbol of ultramodernism.

The neoliberals have built up an extremely effective memetic framework, based on a slogan repeated over and over again, first by Margaret Thatcher, then accepted as a simple truth: *There is no alternative*. There is no alternative to the principles of neoliberalism, and everyone, supporters and opponents alike, must adapt to its norms. The second key lies in the deliberate confusion between "liberalism" and "neoliberalism". The term *liberal* benefits from the positive connotations of its French origins in the Age of Enlightenment; it smacks of Rousseau, Condorcet and Voltaire. The choice of this term constitutes a semantic screen whose status is the result of what sociologist Pierre Bourdieu calls a "gigantic allodoxia", i.e. the rhetorical tactic of mistaking one thing for another. In this logic, everyone is deluded, those who believe as well as those who don't. Originally formulated as a utopia, neoliberalism quickly became "a strong discourse" in the sense of Erving Goffman's analysis of psychiatric discourse in the asylum[129]. It is a discourse that takes its strength from the power relations it generates: it guides the economic thinking of those who possess economic power, on which it accumulates its own symbolic force. The memetic system thus becomes incontestable, closed in on its own strengths, impossible to combat, as the only possible representation of reality.

---

129. *Cf.* GOFFMAN (Erving), *Études sur la condition sociale des malades mentaux*, Éditions de Minuit, 1968.

7. Journey inside the brain

The workings of the brain have always intrigued people, and not just scientists. This organ is the seat of our intelligence, our memory, our emotions, our perceptions, our ability to think, to apprehend and understand knowledge; it is the place where the mind is located, the quintessence of which is consciousness, the "idea of the idea[130]" so dear to Spinoza. The human brain is certainly the most complicated object in the known universe. It is not an organ like any other, and its mysteries invariably resist the onslaught of science. And can science ever subdue it? For a long time, and perhaps still today for some, it was thought that consciousness and the mind could not be the subject of scientific study. Dualism kept things separate: on the one hand, matter, the body, physics; on the other, spirit, consciousness and, why not, God. Scientists, who reject all dualism and cling to their materialism, find themselves prey to immense difficulties: the impossibility of approaching consciousness with the methods of experimental science, the superficiality of medical imaging techniques, the reduction of clinical analyses to a few pathological cases, the limits of psychoanalytical speculation and cybernetic perspectives. The mechanism of consciousness is the focus of all attention, but it jealously

---

130. SPINOZA (Baruch), "L'Éthique, II", in *Œuvres complètes*, Gallimard, coll. La Pléiade, 1954.

guards its secrets. What we know for sure is that consciousness is a process, not a thing; it is the dynamic manifestation[131] of the activity of billions of neurons in different areas of the brain. Research efforts to reveal the inner workings of consciousness have been numerous, often contradictory and sometimes disappointing. Since the 1960s, a myriad of theories and schools of thought have emerged, each as diverse as the next, giving rise to hypotheses as if they were certainties, models of thought that were quickly collapsed and replaced by others. Although this book is not the place for a history of the cognitive sciences, it is important to briefly retrace some of the stages[132] before focusing on certain hypotheses that seem to be commonly accepted today, in an attempt to understand how the brain works, how the flows of information that pass through it are organized, how they reside there in the form of memory, or how they flow to other brains.

The cognitive sciences represent intense, systematic and very large-scale currents of research, located essentially in the USA[133] and divided into two main schools of thought: those who believe that the brain is the seat of mechanisms with a logical level of explanation; and those who believe that the level of explanation is essentially neurological. Cognitive neuroscience falls into the latter category. The first cognitive science research center was set up at Harvard in 1960 by two psychologists, George Miller and Jérôme Bruner, who were protesting

---

131. *Cf.* EDELMAN (Gerald M.), *Vaster than the Sky, A New General Theory of the Brain*, Odile Jacob, 2004.

132. For a brief history, see Brigitte CHAMAK's interesting article, "Sciences cognitives et modèles de pensée", in *Sens public*, September 2004.

133. Important contributions to the conceptual structure of the cognitive sciences were made in Europe in the course of the 20th century, notably the phenomenological movement of Husserl and Merleau-Ponty. Although fundamental, this research is virtually absent from the references of Anglo-Saxon cognitivist researchers, who sometimes rediscover its ideas or reintroduce them as novelties. Cf. VARELA (Francisco), *Invitation aux sciences cognitives*, Seuil, 1996.

against the behaviourist approach dominant at the time[134]. For these two researchers, knowledge essentially consists in the manipulation of symbolic representations. This idea developed and reached its apogee in the 1980s, with the work of psychologist Howard Gardner[135]. He had the intuition to combine, within the same core of cognitive science, psychology and a machine considered to be a good model of the human mind: the computer. This idea became so popular that most of the cognitive sciences used the computer as a model for their thinking and objectives. According to this scheme - which lies at the root of all current research in the field of artificial intelligence - our thoughts can be described by a sequence of logical operations, with the human brain functioning like a computer, combining logical operations performed on abstract symbols. In 1983, cognitive psychologist Jerry Fodor postulated that the human mind is made up of modules designed to process, automatically, a very limited type of information[136]. Cognitive faculties would be information-processing modules in the same way as an automaton processes *inputs* and produces *outputs*. As cyberneticians had done before them in the 1940s[137], cognitivists use the metaphor of Turing's machine as a model of thought and the brain. In 1936, Alan Turing, the brilliant mathematician considered to be the father of modern computing[138], imagined a theoretical device capable of solving all problems in the

---

134. Behaviorism consisted in studying behaviors in relation to the stimuli that triggered them, with no concern for internal mental mechanisms relegated to the famous "black box".
135. *Cf.* GARDNER (Howard), *History of the Cognitive Revolution. The new science of the mind*, Payot, 1993.
136. Cf. FODOR (Jerry A.), *The Modularity of the Mind*, Éditions de Minuit, 1986.
137. For an overview of cybernetic theories from this period, see DUPUY (Jean-Pierre), *Aux origines des sciences cognitives*, La Découverte, 1999.
138. Alan Turing met a dramatic end: victim of prejudice against his homosexuality, he committed suicide in 1954 by biting into an apple impregnated with cyanide. Today, this apple appears as an emblem on millions of computers worldwide, in tribute to his memory.

form of algorithms. According to him, thought is based on logical calculation, so that it is not specific to humans: a machine could very well, if correctly programmed, reproduce the mechanisms of human thought. We can then imagine building computers that "think" simply because they have a list of instructions. A machine may be able to hold a conversation with a human being without the latter knowing whether he or she is conversing with a human or a robot. We can smile or cry at such reductionism. Yet it lies at the root of the tremendous development of computing, which is nothing other than the projection of man's encephalization: after having unloaded his hand, technology is now unloading his brain. The computer's "memory" is already an extension of our memory, and a significant part of our daily lives is already dependent on intelligent machines, autonomous in their decision-making procedures and capable of regulatory procedures. However, none of these machines is yet capable of performing complex tasks as efficiently as the brain. You're reading this book - attentively, I hope. But a sudden noise makes you look up. You turn to the window, trying to understand the nature of the sound that has interrupted your reading. This simple sequence of actions translates into hundreds of thousands of near-simultaneous operations that travel from the eye via the cortex to the hypothalamus. Today, no machine is capable of managing such a profusion of data on a global scale. The *Deep Blue* supercomputer beats world chess champion Kasparov because the machine has the material capacity to anticipate a greater number of moves on the chessboard. However, reproducing the more complex elements of consciousness is problematic. Indeed, if a machine is equipped with sufficiently complex algorithms, it can hold a conversation, but it won't understand the meaning of the words it uses, because it's isolated from the world. Indeed, cognition belongs to beings who live in the world. Neuropsychologist and philosopher Francisco Varela explains this situation well: "The brain exists in a body, the body exists in the world, and the organism acts, moves, hunts, reproduces, dreams, imagines. And it is from this permanent activity that the meaning of its world and things[139] emerge."

In the early 1980s, another school of thought emerged: *connectionism*. This theory has its origins in the work of two cyberneticians, Warren Mc Culloch and Walter Pitts, who in 1943 developed the formal network model. According to this model, neurons are organized in networks; their biological and chemical characteristics are left aside, as they behave like "threshold devices". This means they can be active or inactive, open or closed, like switches, letting current through according to the impulses that excite or inhibit them. In this school of thought, the cognitive system is reduced to a set of relatively simple components, in which deductive logic has no business. It is the interaction between micro-units of information that gives rise to thought. In the cognitivist model, there is a control center that sequentially carries out calculations; in the connectionist approach, calculations are carried out in parallel, without central control, by the simple effect of interactions at neuron level. In line with this idea, Jean-Pierre Changeux was undoubtedly one of the first French scientists to evoke the idea of the transmission of "mental objects[140]" in neural circuits; ideas would thus be objects, potentially observable in neural networks. At any given moment, millions of mental objects are being formed, organized and dissolved in the brain. As a good connectionist, the philosopher Daniel Dennett[141] rejects the idea that these mental objects are controlled by an organizing center that would be in command and manage, behind its dashboard, the various sensory-motor or associative commands. On the contrary, each of these mental objects is constantly at the heart of a competition that bears an uncanny resemblance to Darwinian competition.

---

139. VARELA (Francisco), "Le cerveau n'est pas un ordinateur", interview with Hervé Kempf in *La Recherche*, n° 308, April 1998.
140. CHANGEUX (Jean-Pierre), *L'Homme neuronal*, Fayard, 1983.
141. Cf. DENNETT ((Daniel), *Consciousness Explained*, Odile Jacob, 1993.

Gerald Edelman, director of the *Neuroscience Institute* in San Diego, California, was awarded the Nobel Prize in Medicine in 1972 for his research in immunology. Today, he is working on what is known in journalistic shorthand as "neuronal Darwinism" and, more precisely, the theory of neuronal group selection. This research opens up particularly interesting avenues for understanding, from a biological point of view, how our perception of information from the outside world is structured and what processes we use to form concepts. According to this theory[142], the human genome cannot materially carry the complexity of instructions required to form our neural map. The thirty thousand genes in our genetic make-up would be incapable of managing the architecture of the tens of billions of neuronal connections that make up our cerebral map. The latter can only be formed through a selective construction process, which enables the brain to constantly improve its performance. For Edelman, neurons connect randomly at the embryonic stage. At this early stage of nervous system maturation, nerve cell extensions[143] grow randomly in all directions. This creates billions of synaptic connections, linking billions of neurons to each other in infinitely complex and varied circuits. As the number of synaptic contact points far exceeds the number of genes in the chromosomes, these contacts are not controlled genetically, but by a process that is essentially random[144]. Then, as development progresses, connections become more systematic, depending on the constraints of development itself and the environment. According to this hypothesis, the brain is not "pre-wired", as a computer might be, and has no pre-specified mapping. Only gradually do basic circuits stabilize,

---

142. Cf. EDELMAN (Gerald D.M.) & TONONI (Giulio), *Comment la matière devient conscience*, Odile Jacob, 2001.
143. Cylindraxes.
144. Biologist Jacques Ruffié points out that, at this stage, only the general dispositions of neurons are genetically controlled. Everything else remains free and random, within a fairly broad "genetic envelope". *Op. cit.*

and then groups of circuits assemble and connect to each other to form neuronal "maps". This process continues until birth. After birth, when the young human is in contact with his environment, the sensory organs enable him to form a new organization, which also responds to selection, this time resulting from experience, learning or education. The most-used connections are strengthened, while the least-used gradually disappear. The factors behind the selective stabilization of synapses are first and foremost primary biological forces, such as the need for food or reproduction, but also the individual's material and social environment. Edelman calls these forces *values*, a term that has nothing to do with "values" in the moral sense, but rather with the fundamental needs of a living being. Consciousness is thus a property of biological systems that emerged in the course of evolution, generated by Darwinian mechanisms of natural selection. Francisco Varela explains that it probably results from the evolutionary elaboration of a strategy specific to the animal that must feed itself and, to do so, move and hunt; in other words, implement information flows enabling interactions between perceptions and actions. The cellular links that produce this flow of information constitute an embryonic brain, and "it was on this basis that more abstract things began to be grafted[145]". Between maturation and adulthood, however, neuronal connections are lost. Only useful circuits remain, while others disappear forever. Education thus leads to a paradoxically regressive result: it depletes the number of synapses and reduces the number of nerve circuits in use. This is why young subjects are more easily educated than older individuals, with learning abilities tending to diminish as the number of available neural circuits decreases. It's also worth noting that this phenomenon provides some instruction for the old debate on innate and acquired. There are innate behaviors that correspond to fundamental activities, necessary for the survival of the individual. These behaviours are not formed at random,

---

145. VARELA (Francisco), interview with Hervé Kempf, *op. cit.*

but are directly dependent on genetic information. On the other hand, acquired experiences, such as those acquired through education, are only formed at certain points in development, and are preferentially assimilated according to fixed sequences. Acquired experience, particularly of memetic origin, is thus accommodated within a pre-established structure, which is in turn innate.

The brain described by Edelman is the seat of extremely complex neuronal wiring, allowing an immense number of synaptic connections[146]. There are 1 million billion of them. This number may not mean much to you, but if you count all the synaptic connections, one per second, it would take no less than 32 million years to complete. These connections occur in many different places, and simultaneously. The selected circuits form what Edelman calls neural maps. These maps, which are massively interconnected, will in turn be able to associate by entering into temporal "resonance". Millions of neurons are thus activated in parallel, informing each other. It is from this constant flow of neuronal impulses that perception, and then conceptual thought, are constructed. Let's try to understand this complex mechanism: when a stimulus - internal or external, it doesn't matter - is received by the organism, different neuronal maps are excited at the same time. I see an object, for example; at that moment and simultaneously, neuronal maps are activated, one for the object's color, another for its texture, a third for its functionality, and so on. A sensory system such as vision requires the operation of some thirty neuronal maps, distributed throughout the brain. These neural maps are not coordinated by a central operator, a kind of vision computer program. It's their interaction that allows me to say that this object belongs to such and such a category, and that it has such and such a use. You understand that the neural maps triggered by the object in question are my own. When you perceive the same object, you will

---

146. 1 mm^3 of gray matter in the cortex can contain 5 billion synapses.

have other neural maps, certainly very different from mine, which will be activated according to the context. Neural connectivity is a function of each individual's own experience; moreover, it varies throughout his or her life according to the new experiences he or she has acquired. What's important to understand is that the complex mechanism I'm describing takes place in milliseconds. What's more, the richer the individual's experience, the greater the number of neuronal maps that "switch on" at the same time, and the finer his or her consciousness[147].

You will readily admit that the system Edelman describes is far more complex than that of the behaviourists or the computer of the computationalists, whose causality is simple and linear: a cause generates an effect, in a defined way, by simple association. Consciousness, the product of millions of years of evolution, does not function as a simple receiving mechanism. It's a complex system. In such a system, the sheer mass of variables - billions of neurons, each with thousands of synapses - makes it impossible to predict the system's future states.

At this point in our journey to the center of the brain, it's natural, if you're a little curious, to ask the question that Edelman doesn't fully answer: how does this multitude of information pass through the neurons? By what miracle is the brain able to process so much data so quickly, and at the same time?

Edelman believes that chemicals such as neurotransmitters play a key role in neuronal communication. Let's not forget that Edelman was originally a specialist in immunology, which is why his model closely resembles the way the immune system develops its ability to "recognize" certain substances. However, as they are understood, these processes are handled in a classical algorithmic way, reproducible quite easily by computers[148]. Some researchers are convinced that this

---

147. *Cf.* EDELMAN (Gerald M.), *Vaster than the Sky. A new general theory of the brain, op. cit.*
148. Gerald Edelman and his colleagues have developed a whole series of digitally controlled devices (called Darwin I, II, III, etc.) which simulate, in order of increasing complexity, the procedures that are supposed to form the basis of mental activity.

assimilation of brain function to a process that can be controlled like a computer does not reflect the reality of the activity of the conscious mind. The work of the world-renowned British mathematician and physicist, Sir Roger Penrose, builds on this critique to shed a particularly innovative light on brain function. According to him, the procedures that bring synaptic connections into play cannot be calculated using conventional algorithms, as they are based on a physical process that is in the realm of complex systems, in which quantum coherence plays a decisive role. To further our investigation, I'm obliged to ask you to follow me into a completely original and particularly intriguing field of research, that of quantum consciousness. Rest assured, I'm no mathematician, and even less capable of understanding all the intricacies of quantum computation, so we'll confine ourselves to outlining the broad outlines of this work, which is already instructive enough for our purpose.

Penrose's intuition began with the apparently simple observation of a humble paramecium under the microscope[149]. This little bug, well known to young schoolchildren making their first forays into the world of micro-organisms, moves around in its culture broth thanks to innumerable cilia that surround it like hair. It pounces on any food it detects and flees at the slightest danger. What's more, it seems able to avoid obstacles by going around them, as if learning from past experience. Yet the paramecium has neither neurons nor synapses. How can it accomplish all this? Paramecium's behavior is identical to that of all living unicellular organisms: it is governed not by a central nervous system like ours, but by a structure responsible for control: the cytoskeleton. As its name suggests, this is the framework that structures the entire cell. But the cytoskeleton doesn't just act as a kind of carapace, it performs a host of other functions; in fact, the cytos-

---

149. *Cf.* PENROSE (Roger), *Les Ombres de l'esprit. In Search of a Science of Consciousness,* InterÉditions, 1995.

keleton is a veritable gift-wrapping package, comprising the muscular system, the locomotor system, the circulatory system and the nervous system all rolled into one. Why are we interested in the cytoskeleton of paramecia? Because *our* neurons are themselves individual cells with their own cytoskeleton. This could lead us to believe that each neuron in our brain is itself endowed with a "personal nervous system". This is a particularly fascinating avenue that many researchers are passionately exploring[150]. Penrose, too, took a close look at two of the cytoskeleton's structural components: microtubules and intermediate filaments. Microtubules are hollow cylindrical tubes of around 25 nm^2 in diameter[151], sometimes grouped into fibers organized in a characteristic geometric pattern reminiscent of a merry-go-round of wooden horses. Each microtubule is itself made up of sub-units, the tubulins, resembling peanuts in a hexagonal network running the length of the tube. These little objects have different geometric configurations (conformations) corresponding to two states of electrical polarization, rather like a miniature electronic switch. The control center of the cytoskeleton, if such a term can be used at all, is a particular structure: the centriole, which resembles a disjoint T formed by two bundles of microtubules. I won't go into the details of how this centriole works, but I would like to emphasize an interesting point: the presence of this control organ suggests that there are two "headquarters" within a single cell: the nucleus, which we know well, as it is the seat of the cell's genetic heritage; but there is also the centriole, which plays an organizing role. Why two control centers? At the start of this book, I introduced you to biologist Lynn Margulis. She explained that certain primitive prokaryotic cells were visited by foreign organisms - notably spirochaetes - and learned to live in symbiosis with them. Spirochaetes

---

150. *Cf.* Hameroff (Stuart R.), *Ultimate Computing: Biomolecular Consciousness and Nanotechnology*, Elsevier Science Ltd, 1987.
151. Nm = nanometer = 10^{-9} m = 0.000 000 000 1 meter.

possess a cytoskeleton which, despite billions of years of evolution, has remained at the heart of our cells. In particular, our nerve cells. This is why these cells have two control centers: one evolved, the nucleus; the other of more primitive origin, the centriole. What's the significance of this discovery? It's of the utmost importance, because it reveals that the microtubules in our neurons act as "cellular automata[152]", processing and transmitting complex signals along the tubes. These signals are said to be waves caused by differences in polarization of the tubulins, those little peanuts I've been telling you about. Another interesting aspect of this discovery is that it considerably increases our brain's computing power, which was already thought to be very high. Hans Moravec, one of the leading authorities on artificial intelligence, thought that our brains were capable, in principle, of performing some 10^{14} fundamental operations per second, but no more than[153]. This figure is already very high, since it represents a number made up of fourteen zeros. If we accept, as Penrose does, that tubulins play a major role in the brain, then computing power rises to 10^{27} operations per second. The world's most powerful computers achieve, according to Moravec, a power comparable to the first value of 10^{14}; on the other hand, they seem to have no hope of reaching the 10^{27} operations per second of the human brain in the foreseeable future. Of course, we must temper our enthusiasm and pride, as the human brain never uses its capacities to 100%. It is clear, however, that the possibility of "microtubular computing" casts a pall over the ambitions of artificial intelligence to one day match the human brain.

But what is the point of this race for computing power? Why should we be endowed with such prodigious calculators? Penrose believes that the reason is not the one we spontaneously expect: to do more

---

152. PENROSE (Roger), *op. cit.*
153. MORAVEC (Hans), *Mind Children: The Future of Robot and Human Intelligence*, Harvard University Press, 1990.

operations and calculations. The mechanism that governs our brain is not based on the same model as a calculator, but is rather the seat of a large-scale quantum coherence phenomenon operating in microtubules. We saw a moment ago that microtubules can behave like "waveguides", transmitting signals along their tubes. These dielectric waves have such a high frequency of quantum oscillation that, theoretically, they can only travel in a vacuum. But what's inside these tubes? There's no vacuum, but there is water. Logically, water interferes with the circulation of quantum waves because, with its molecules animated by random movements, it is not sufficiently organized to allow quantum waves to evolve normally. Yes, but the water in our cells isn't just any water; it's not the water in your tap or in the ocean. It's "vicinal" water, which has the particularity of producing an ordered state of its molecules. As a result, this water is highly conducive to the presence of coherent quantum oscillations inside the tubes. The microtubules would then be the seat of considerable quantum activity. Not only does this activity extend along the entire length of the microtubule, but it can also extend to other neighboring microtubules, helping to form quantum coherence in the neuron cytoskeleton. Moreover, this quantum coherence must cross the synaptic barrier separating two neurons to truly speak of global coherence extending to large parts of the brain. This passage to other neurons defies the laws of classical biology. And yet, it seems proven that this feat is possible. Based on the work of German physicist Henry Margenau[154], renowned neurophysiologist John Eccles emphasizes the importance of quantum effects in synaptic activity. In his view, certain brain cells[155] are indeed the seat of quantum activity. He states: "The mind/brain interaction is analogous to a probability field described in quantum mechanics, a field

---

154. He states: "We can think of the mind as a field in the physical sense of the word. But as a non-material field, perhaps its closest analogy is with a probability field." MARGENAU (Henry), *Miracle of Existence*, Ox Bow Pr., 1984.
155. In particular, the presynaptic vesicular grid.

that has no mass or energy and can, however, in a microsite, cause an action that has effects[156]." Penrose observes that there are two closely interwoven and congruent networks: a biological network of neuronal cells, communicating via synapses, and a quantum network, involving the neuronal cytoskeleton and operating by instantaneous integration of a superposition of states. The first network would interact with the second via the neuromediators that shape the cytoskeleton; the second would interact with the first via the orchestrated selection of spacetimes[157] that would modify the electrical charge of the neurons it involves.

This research leads us to deduce that human consciousness results from the interplay of a quantum network and a biological network. The first network is the scene of the connection, rigorously simultaneous with each reduction in state, of a vast population of neuronal cells. It would seem, then, that the quantum network is activated by the majority of mental operations when it comes to integrating disparate elements: operations of synthesis, comprehension, associations of ideas, and so on. In the phenomenon known as comprehension, for example, a sometimes extremely considerable amount of data is integrated that didn't make sense the moment before - to the point where it's often referred to as a "flash of comprehension". All these operations that we usually associate with intellectual alertness are, to a large extent, the result of quantum integration. The second network, biological and genetically determined, is the privileged medium by which the individual defines himself, outside any memory or environment. This network is dense and diffuse - ten thousand synapses per neuron - polarized and slow. Its processes are inscribed in time, and it is this network that gives rhythm to thought and subjective temporality. The inter-neuronal connection network,

---

156. Eccles (John C.), *op. cit.*
157. Orchestrated space-time selection.

slowly built up by experience and memory input - and partly by genetic code - defines preferred ways and methods of processing and routing information, so that a pathway that once led to the resolution of a problem is facilitated when a similar problem is encountered, following the classic mechanism of reinforcing synaptic connections. But the determination of these similarities is left to the quantum side, which alone is capable of integrating all of the intellect's information, freeing itself from these same pathways and methods. As we can see, human rational reasoning is based on a dialogue, a permanent back-and-forth that leads from quantum integration to the linear, experimental processing of the results of this integration by the biological intellect. Quantum integration is instantaneous, but takes place without method or restraint; the biological path is constructed, but linear and devoid of perspective.

Penrose's contribution and the analysis of these two interlocking networks complement Edelman's hypotheses and highlight a hitherto unexplored property of human consciousness: that of giving rise to a second universe in its own right, whose field of quantum simultaneity is space, and whose subjective biological temporality is time. Together, they form a specific informational space-time, unique to each conscious subject. This complex system belongs to the field of chaos. It is made up of a very large number of neurons and possible connections. It does not obey a set list of instructions, but can adjust to incoming information; this is its adaptive function. It can also create information by instantly organizing the chaos of the neuronal system in a new space-time; this is its self-organizing function. Using its own resources, the network generates information without being stimulated, which is only possible in a system with non-linear dynamics. This characteristic enables creative activity that manifests itself as interpretation, dreaming, emotion or imagination; it's the mutation function. System evolutions are unpredictable, which is the very nature of chaotic systems. Chaos is what enables a system to evolve and create; it's highly likely that our neural network functions in this way: our imagination, the thread of our thoughts, is a dynamic that requires chaotic organization to create information; our conscious activity is not just a device that varies according to the surrounding state, as functionalism might have suggested; it's a dynamic that interprets, is moved, imagines, anticipates, in its own temporal universe. This is the meaning of Nietzsche's premonitory formula: "You have to carry chaos inside you to give birth to a dancing star[158]".

Penrose's theories are naturally very appealing, but like all innovative scientific hypotheses, they are also controversial. In particular, they are criticized for composing a kind of neo-dualism that would establish more or less well-defined bridges between mind and matter. Other critics, general to most new neuroscience theories, regret that the individual's free will is often left out of the equation. Some researchers, for example, have exhumed the notion of intentionality forged by Saint Thomas Aquinas in the 13th century. Such is the case of Walter Freeman[159], who believes that the brain is involved in processes of intentionality, creating meanings in the form of symbols, gestures or words. These meanings are implemented by the brain, which modifies its neural mappings according to the consequences these meanings will have on the environment or on others. Taking up Piaget's principle of "assimilation"[160], Freeman believes that human beings understand the world by adapting to it, through a continuous process of feedback. Freeman's "meanings" are living structures that emerge, develop and evolve. I think the word "meaning" must illuminate a neural map in you that has something to do with the memes we talked about in earlier chapters. You might have imagined that

---

158. NIETZSCHE (Friedrich), *Ainsi parlait Zarathoustra*, Mercure de France, 1952.
159. FREEMAN (Walter J.), *How Brains Make up Their Minds*, Columbia University Press, 2001.
160. PIAGET (Jean), *La Naissance de l'intelligence chez l'enfant (1936)*, Delachaux et Niestle, 1992 and *La Représentation du monde chez l'enfant (1947)*, PUF, 2003.

by delving into the mysteries of brain theories, we'd get rid of them, but memes are back in the limelight, with the theses of Cambridge anthropologist and biologist Robert Aunger.

Robert Aunger gives some particularly interesting extensions to the various theories we've just mentioned. Taking up Edelman's hypotheses on neuronal Darwinism, he considers that the cerebral operations resulting from the functioning of neurons do indeed follow an evolutionary process. At first, they are limited to sensory-motor relations, then, as the individual develops, they are enriched by new functionalities resulting from a multiplication of connections between neurons and synapses, a proliferation generated by learning, experience and imitation. According to Aunger[161], the bridges between synapses and neurons that ensure brain plasticity are built by what he calls *neuromemes*. Neuromemes play a major role in the brain, triggering the neuronal maps described by Edelman. For Aunger, these are physical realities that may one day be identified by advances in brain imaging. In line with Penrose's theories on quantum consciousness, Aunger believes that neuromemes embody a coherence of state between several neurons, at a given time and place in the brain, thus triggering the production of a global impulse. The neuromeme is then understood as the configuration of a neuronal network node, capable of creating impulses in other network nodes, notably through replication. These neuromemes can be extremely numerous, since each of the tens of billions of neurons in the human brain can generate one at any given moment. Some of these neuromemes are static, located in relatively stable areas of the brain, while others are highly mobile, associating with each other and acting simultaneously in several different areas of the brain, and in particular in the different memories it contains. Neuromemes thus constitute the individual's cultural personality,

---

161. Cf. Aunger (Robert), *The Electric Meme. A New Theory of How we Think*, Cambridge, The Free Press, 2002.

mobile bricks of cognitive content, migrating from one area of the brain to another and from our short-term memory to our long-term memory. Circulating in the nervous system from neuron to neuron, neuromemes enter into Darwinian competition with one another, but more often than not they also associate with one another, forming more or less stable ensembles. These sets - which Aunger calls "meta-memes" - correspond to the establishment of representations of the environment and the individual's situation within it. These representations are stable, even permanent references, enabling the individual to situate himself in time, understand his past, interpret his present and orient his future.

Aunger's description of how memes work in our brains is certainly open to criticism, but it has the merit of being fairly consistent with previous theories. However, if she describes relatively well what's going on inside our brains, how does she explain a fundamental characteristic of memes, which I've already mentioned: they jump from brain to brain. How could memes escape from my brain to contaminate - or enrich - yours? How can we explain the transmission of memes?

To answer this question, Aunger uses the concept of *instigator*[162]. But before we go any further, we need to get rid of a baroque idea: a meme doesn't "literally" jump from brain to brain, like a small bug would do to contaminate a neighboring organism. The meme cannot be directly replicated identically; nor is it concealed, as such, within signals that the individual might emit. As anthropologist and cognitive scientist Dan Sperber, a specialist in the epidemiology of representations, clearly states: signals do not contain thoughts, which always remain inside the brain[163]. They are private representations of the world and

---

162. "Instigator." *Cf. The Electric Meme, op. cit.*
163. Cf. SPERBER (Dan), "An Objection to the Memetic Approach to Culture", in *Darwinizing Culture: The Status of Memetics as a Science*, Robert AUNGER (ed.), Oxford University Press, 2000.

our imaginary world. So, the meme itself cannot be transmitted to someone else; on the other hand, it can perfectly well emit, via the brain it hosts, signals of a certain type, destined for another human brain. At a primary stage of evolution, these "instigator" signals are emitted automatically, regardless of the presence or absence of a possible receiver. In this case, they are emitted in the same way as a plant diffuses its fragrance, without worrying about which organism will receive it and be stimulated. When another brain receives this instigator, it triggers an internal process enabling the creation of a counterpart to the original meme. The meme's lineage then continues to evolve as if no space had been crossed between individuals. But the work doesn't stop there, as the transmitted meme undergoes a process of construction or reconstruction in the receiving brain. The latter contains other memes which compete with the newcomer, rejecting or distorting it, or assimilating and integrating it. The role of instigating signals, in this perspective, is not to carry any information in the copy of the meme, but rather to create the conditions for a local transformation, resulting in the copy or replication of the emitted meme. If I tell you "apple", I'm sending you a signal that will trigger a large amount of information in your brain corresponding to the idea you have of an apple. You'll think of fruit, summer, tarte Tatin, Adam and Eve, a tangy taste, a color, whatever... A large number of neural maps will certainly light up in your mind. When your brain receives the *apple* signal, it doesn't make a meme out of it; it converts the instigating signal into a neural state, making the meme present. The instigator signal thus fulfils a minimal role: that of triggering information enabling replication. What's important to understand is that the relationship between the instigator and the meme is totally arbitrary, since the instigator contains no part of the meme. He has merely triggered the "ignition" of a certain number of neural maps, i.e. meanings in which the meme has replicated itself. To get the meme from one brain to the other, the instigating signals are elaborated with the means available, first and foremost those under the control of the motor neurons available to the body: gestures, then speech, then the artifacts that mankind will constantly invent throughout its evolution. In the receiving brain, the meme circulates via electrochemical exchanges and possibly quantum oscillations between cerebral neurons. I explained the mechanism to you not long ago.

For the instigating signal to be transmitted and received, a minimum number of conditions must be met. These are the classic conditions of communication. One of these is that the organisms exchanging memes via the initiating signals must have similarities. Some of these are genetically programmed. Noam Chomsky, whom we have already met in a previous chapter, asserts that language exists in man because certain genetically programmed structures are already present; we would thus possess the "language instinct" says Stephen Pinker. There is thus a "human nature[164]", i.e. a set of traits shared by all human beings. These traits, the product of genetic evolution, constitute the originality of our species, a kind of universal foundation built up since the dawn of time. In other cases, for communication to take place, a certain number of evolutionary developments must have been generated in order to establish a community of life or thought. In this case, memes intervene at the margins of what already exists. They don't build from nothing; they need a pre-existing substrate to be able to trigger meanings. Just as physics has its elementary particles, chemistry its elements, genetics the four nucleic acids of DNA, just as a language can say anything by arranging some thirty phonemes, so each culture combines a certain number of symbolic universals. These are the source of the inexhaustible combination of arrangements, permutations and rearrangements that give rise to cultural diversity. Communication is only possible because people have common mental structures, common "modules" in the terminology of evolutionary psychologists.

---

164. Pinker (Steven), *Understanding Human Nature*, Odile Jacob, 2005.

If you've never seen an apple in your life, the word *apple* won't mean a thing to you. That's why I'm inclined to think that "culture" is a similarity rather than a sharing. Indeed, when a meme, understood as a unit of cultural information, is disseminated in a human group, it spreads to different brains, but is never shared between these different brains. If the meme remains stable in the group, it's because it benefits from a particular interest or is particularly robust and "contagious". This is one of the reasons why we speak of Darwinian selection for memes: those that survive are those that are adapted to the environment that receives them, or that impose themselves as an advantage in the sense that evolutionary theory might understand it. These memes are the different ways in which brains represent the world; they build what Edelman calls a "second nature[165]", i.e. the body of individual and collective knowledge - be it scientific, technical, metaphorical or symbolic - that enables man to live in his environment, evolve with others, and project himself into the world.

---

165. Edelman (Gerald M.), *Second Nature. Brain, Science and Human Knowledge*, Yale University Press, 2007.

Interlude VII

Bionic dream or Promethean nightmare?

Matthew Naggle is a 26-year-old American who had the misfortune to be stabbed in the neck during a common street fight. He was left a quadriplegic. His name won't go down in the annals of countless similar incidents. By contrast, Matthew Naggle was the first human being to control a computer by thought. He is the first man to establish a connection between neuron and electron.

It's not telepathy, but a technological feat achieved by John Donoghue's team at Rhode Island's Brown University[166]. An electronic component measuring 4 mm on a side and bristling with a hundred electrodes has been implanted in the region of his brain that controls voluntary movements. This component picks up electrical signals from neurons and transmits them, via a cable connected to the young American's skull, to computers which analyze the nerve impulses and translate them into animated pixels. With his mind, Matthew Naggle is able to move a cursor on a computer screen and control the movements of a hand and an artificial arm. The researchers who achieved this feat believe they are just at the beginning of a dream: to directly control the tetraplegic's muscles using his brain signals.

---

166. Cf. *Nature*, July 13, 2006.

The medical benefits of such experimentation are immense. Reconnecting the disconnected or broken links between mind and body, between the real and the virtual, through the intermediary of an electronic device opens up hope to all those for whom, like Matthew Naggle, only their brain activity remains to survive.

However, this news deserves to go beyond the euphoria of scientific and medical discovery, and question the strange nature of this hybridization between technologies and the human body. The body, virtualized, escapes its reality and the boundaries of its biological organization. The virtual body is the fantasy of the Golem, the world of robots and androids. Long confined to the imagination of science-fiction writers, these fields are now taking over research laboratories the world over. For a long time now, the Western world has been approaching robotization from an industrial angle, with the aim of improving productivity and lightening the burden of arduous human tasks. Assembly lines in all industrial sectors are automated and robotized. Robots perform technical and mechanical functions. From other horizons and cultures, the robot takes on another dimension. In Japan, robotics research is working on machines capable of performing anthropoid functions. With its culture and religion detached from the taboo of the Golem, Japan is neither intellectually nor ethically limited in the increasingly perfect reproduction of the human being. Accompanying robots, new virtual confidants, are emerging from the research centers of Honda, Mitsubishi and Sony.

In the arts, robot dancers are appearing on major choreographic stages. Numerous experiments are being conducted, the fruit of collaboration between choreographers and cybernetic engineers. They reveal both the attraction and repulsion that body-substituting technologies can represent for artists whose body is the sacred medium of expression and creativity. Today, dancers no longer hesitate to let their bodies be absorbed by machines. The experience of choreographer

Marcel Li Antunez and his exoskeleton is interesting in this respect: the dancer is "incarcerated" in a robot whose movements are dictated in particular by those of the audience. For the artist, the interactivity produced poses the problem of the painful double constraint: that of man on man, but also that of the machine on man. Other artists investigate the field of body splitting, creating performances in which the dancers' bodies are alternately, but simultaneously, real and virtual.

8. The projected man

Until very recently, common sense agreed with the assertions of scientific theory, which maintained, as if it were a natural thing, that communication between two human beings consists in the linking of two brains considered as information-processing machines. This technicist conception, developed in the 1950s by the famous Claude Shannon and Warren Weaver[167], is still adopted today in computer science, artificial intelligence and even linguistics. The scheme is very simple - not to say "simplistic": a message emitted by the source is, once encoded, propagated through a physical channel to a receiver, who decodes it. If communication between humans were that simple, we'd have known about it a long time ago. But it isn't. The brain is not a simple computer fed with coded information, nor can sender and receiver be reduced to simple devices for transmitting and receiving information. Neurophysiologists have clearly demonstrated that the communication of ideas through language cannot be reduced to the simple decoding of a linguistic signal. Words trigger highly complex signals that activate groups of specific neural maps that vary from one individual to another. This is why Chomsky was able to observe considerable discrepancies between the possible poverty of a stimulus

---

167. SHANNON (Claude E.) & WEAVER (Warren), *The Mathematical Theory of Communication*, Chicago, Illinois University Press, 1949.

emitted by a speaker and the wealth of internal knowledge that sets in motion in the receiver's head. A simple word can set off a storm in a skull, with devastating or wonderfully evocative effects.

What's more, the communication of ideas requires a "mediating system[168]", i.e. a common base of knowledge that interlocutors enrich, and from which they inform each other. However, Dan Sperber and Deirdre Wilson go even further, arguing that communication involves the sender *transforming* the "cognitive environment[169]" of the interlocutor's brain. When I talk to you, I try to modify the assumptions that are present in your brain, so that you accept as true those that I communicate to you. But you don't remain passive, and in order to maximize communication, you'll try to recognize my intentions. So, when we communicate, you and I have in our heads a vast amount of information of all kinds, which constitutes our mental state. So communication can't be reduced to a simple in-and-out scheme. Jean-Pierre Changeux believes that, "in line with the thesis that the brain operates in a projective style, making use of contextualized pre-representations, we can assume that each speaker is constantly trying to *project* his frame of thought into the head of his interlocutor[170]." In communication, man projects himself, and this projection involves connecting to the brains of others. This is the prerequisite not only for communication, but also for social and cultural life. How is this possible?

In 1996, a group of neurologists from the University of Parma in Italy, led by Giacomo Rizzolati, made a discovery that is considered a veritable scientific revolution: that of *mirror neurons.* The Director of the *Center for Brain and Cognition* at the University of California is no exception, exclaiming: "The discovery of mirror neurons is the

---

168. VYGOTSKY (Lev), *Thought and Language*, Cambridge, MIT Press, 1986.
169. SPERBER (Dan) & WILSON (Deirdre), *Relevance: Communication and Cognition*, 2nd edition, Blackwell Publishers, 1995.
170. CHANGEUX (Jean-Pierre), *L'Homme de vérité, op. cit.* (emphasis added).

most important news of the decade. I predict that mirror neurons will do for psychology what DNA did for biology[171]." Mirror neurons are neurons that activate not only when the individual performs an action, but also when he watches a fellow human perform the same action. Initial research was carried out on monkeys. Using brain imaging, scientists noticed that neurons located in a specific area of the premotor cortex[172] were activated when the monkey performed a specific movement, such as grabbing a piece of fruit. Surprisingly, however, the same neurons were activated when the monkey did not perform the movement, but simply *observed* the same gesture being performed by another person, be it a monkey or the experimenter. There is therefore a direct relationship between action and observation[173]. The same mirror neurons exist in humans, but in a much more highly developed form. Observations made on humans, particularly young children, have shown that these neurons are directly linked to the learning and imitation process. They enable us not only to imitate, but also to discover the *intentions taking* place in the brain of the person we are observing. Let's take a concrete example, proposed by Giacomo Rizzolati himself: "John is watching Mary pick a flower. John not only knows what Mary is doing - she's picking the flower - but he also knows why she's doing it. As she smiles at him, he guesses that she's about to offer him the flower. This scene lasts a few seconds, and Jean understands it almost instantly. How can he effortlessly conceive Mary's precise action and intention[174]?" A decade

171. Ramachandran (Vilayanur S.), "Mirror Neurons and Imitation Learning as the Driving Force behind 'the Great Leap forward' in Human Evolution", in *Edge 69*, June 1st, 2000 (online at: www.edge.org/documents/archive/edge69.html).
172. These neurons were first detected in area F5 of the premotor cortex, then also in the rostral part of the inferior parietal lobe. These neurons are found in humans and certain birds.
173.. Cf. Rizzolati (Giacomo) *et al*, "Premotor Cortex and the Recognition of Motor Actions", in *Cognitive Brain Research*, n° 3, 1996, p. 131-141.
174. Rizzolati (Giacomo), "Les neurones miroirs", in *Pour la Science*, n° 351, January 2007.

or so ago, most neurobiologists and psychologists would have attributed a person's understanding of others' actions, and in particular their intentions, to a rapid reasoning process, similar to that used to solve a logical problem: some elaborate cognitive device in John's brain would organize the information transmitted by the senses and compare it with similar memorized experiences, enabling John to guess what Mary is about to do and why. The discovery of mirror neurons explains that, in the observer's brain, there is a "reflection" of the actions and intentions of the person being observed. Mirror neurons literally allow us to *project* ourselves into another person's brain, establishing a form of communication based not on words, language or ideas, but on intentions.

Man is a being of projection. The famous anthropologist Edward T. Hall unequivocally states: "No other species can even remotely compete with man in the accomplishment of his evolution through self-projection[175]". The human brain has a unique characteristic: it functions projectively. It constantly elaborates hypotheses and anticipations about the world, its environment and others. It tries to create stable categories by projecting pre-representations of meaning. He projects models that will become cultures. Of course, inventions, technical innovations and mythologies don't spring spontaneously from a single glance or gesture at reality. These human projections are generally developed slowly, progressively, from small, insignificant, incomplete and sometimes inaudible events, from exchanges and trial and error, imitations, tinkering, mistakes and cooperative encounters. Following on from Dan Sperber's research[176], American philosopher Aaron Lynch speaks of the epidemiology of ideas[177]. A culture could

---

175. HALL (Edward T.), *Beyond Culture*, Seuil, 1979.
176. Cf. SPERBER (Dan), *The Contagion of Ideas*, Odile Jacob, 1996.
177. Cf. LYNCH (Aaron), *Thought Contagion: How Belief Spreads Through Society*, New York, Basic Books, 1996 and "An Introduction to Evolutionary Epidemiology of Ideas", in *The Biological Physicist*, vol. 3, no. 2, 2003, pp. 7-13.

then be identified with a certain distribution of projected ideas within a given population. Indeed, culture is not just a social construct, it is subject to the configurations of individuals' brains, forged by several millennia of evolution. An idea projected by one brain also encounters, in the recipient brain, already shaped cognitive modules that Sperber calls "intuitive beliefs". This is why a small child will more easily learn to distinguish between animals - even if, like giraffes or snakes, it doesn't know them directly - than to integrate the rules of multiplication tables. The child's brain contains mental modules that existed at the time of the first hominids, a time when it was better to recognize animals than to do mental arithmetic, in order to preserve survival. What's more, cultural contents are not replicated as they are; they are modified according to their suitability and relevance, i.e. their ability to ensure maximum cognitive effect with minimum effort. They then form a set of cultural memes that spread throughout a human population, some of them lasting for several generations.

Oral language is the first projection. As I've already mentioned, it was oral language that led to the first great advances of the human species. But as soon as man learned to *write,* his progress became incoercible. In fact, the invention of techniques consisting in marking wooden, stone, bone or clay supports with signs, enabled man to free up his brain's storage capacities and thus increase his faculties of projection onto others and onto the world. The oldest known signs of writing certainly date back to the beginning of the Paleolithic era, 30,000 years ago; they bear witness to man's first faculties of observation, abstraction and documentation. These are engraved bone plates discovered in the 1950s in the French Périgord region[178] and featuring signs representing the successive phases of the moon over several months. The engraver

---

178. On the "Abri Blanchard" and "Abri Lartet" sites in the Eyzies de Tayac region of Périgord.

took care to choose very fine tools to represent the changing shape of the moon through small incisions organized in groups[179]. Nothing comparable has been discovered for the following ten thousand years. In seeking to engrave the cycles of the moon, the human beings of this period, true astronomers before their time, certainly didn't realize that they were breaking new ground. In fact, they had just invented the prototype of writing, i.e. the means of extending human cerebral memory through *artificial projection*. Whether in the form of cuneiform signs, hieroglyphs, Chinese, Aztec or Mayan ideograms, writing is an artificial memory. This first "prosthesis" of the brain will enable the long-term storage of ideas, phenomena, thoughts, information - in a word, memes - destined to be transmitted to other humans, far away in time and space. The genesis of information and communication tools is a perpetual story of research and the implementation of simulacra enabling the emergence, conservation and transmission of traces. Human beings have invented means of communication to transmit and disseminate not only messages, but also their history. But more than that, projection through writing leads man to examine what's in his head and perfect it, "for once something is externalized, we can observe it, study it, change it, perfect it, all the while learning essential things about ourselves[180]." Like a block of marble carved by a sculptor, thought is forged by writing, until it takes shape.

The transition from oral to written transmission of memes was decisive. It marked a stage in the reorganization of the world. Indeed, the written text implies an organization of observations, conjectures and thoughts. The written word not only preserves, but also makes visible and organizes knowledge, and thus the world. The first written traces, engraved on bone, clay or wax, were utilitarian reminders of

---

179. Cf. Marshack (Alexander), *Hierarchical Evolution of the Human Capacity: The Paleolithic Evidence*, New York, American Museum of Natural History, 1985.
180. Hall (Edward T.), *op. cit.*

phenomena, accounts or material goods[181]. Soon enough, however, the written word became a medium for thought and a means of projecting it. Papyrus and ink took over from engraving. Writing was rolled up into *volumen*, scrolls up to ten meters long. Then parchment, less brittle than papyrus, could be folded into *codexes*. Then came paper and the book we know so well. The first *volumen* were very numerous. They had to be preserved in special buildings, the most famous of which was the Library of Alexandria. Its site was only part of a much larger structure, the *Mouseion*, destined to house the entire memory of the world's knowledge: collections of natural objects, techniques and works of art. The work of projecting, preserving and replicating human memory had begun, and nothing could stop it.

The invention of the alphabet was a major innovation with far-reaching consequences. It made it possible to move from ideographic to digital writing, in line with the forms that information takes in nature. Unlike Egyptian hieroglyphs, Mesopotamian cuneiforms, Chinese ideograms or pre-Columbian pictograms, the alphabet is based on a combination of less than thirty signs representing sounds. It thus takes on a universal dimension. Indeed, the ancient signs were confined to the cultures that invented them, independently of each other. However, all the world's current alphabets derive directly from protosinaitic - 1,200 years B.C. - from a handful of hieroglyphs migrated from Egypt, which became the sound carriers of a Semitic language. All alphabets - Phoenician, Hebrew, Arabic, Sanskrit, Greek, Latin and Cyrillic - derive from this initial invention, which was promoted to the rank of the first universal system of communication. Thanks to its simplicity, the alphabet took writing out of the exclusive domain of scribes and spread to all populations. In its wake were born

---

181. Most ancient pictographic writings, notably those found at Uruk, the Sumerian capital, dating back to 3,700 BC, served utilitarian functions: counting animals or foodstuffs, for example. However, ancient engraved bones found in China were probably used by shamans to predict the future.

law, money, philosophy, mathematics and the great religions based on sacred texts written in Hebrew, Greek, Latin, Arabic or Sanskrit alphabetical characters.

One of the purposes of projection is to highlight a particular function of the biological organism. Unlike animals, which are obliged to transform themselves through slow mutations to equip themselves with beaks, claws or wings, man now escapes this servitude and becomes capable of progressing without changing form, of infinitely varying his action, without his genetic coding changing. In *Homo sapiens sapiens*, genetic evolution has reached a plateau. It can be stated with certainty that no further significant evolution of hominids will take place. The last evolutionary stage reached some 100,000 years ago took place in a population representing around 2 million individuals worldwide. Today's human population is more than three thousand times larger. It is therefore highly unlikely that a mutation will escape dilution in humanity's immense genetic reservoir. Of course, we could go back to the collective madness of selecting the fittest, as Hitler fomented for his ideal Aryan society. We could also conceive of biotechnological inventions producing mutations that are as accelerated as they are artificial. But here we are in the realm of science fiction, which is beyond the scope of this article. In this respect, however, we should moderate our previous certainty, and *hope that* no significant genetic evolution of hominids will take place. *Homo sapiens will* remain *sapiens* for a long time to come, but his potential is infinite. Indeed, the realm of memetic evolution has none of the limitations of the biological realm. This is what makes man such a singular animal, but also such a dangerous one.

We can't understand man without studying his projections. Freed from the organism, man's evolution accelerates; his projections have enabled him to dominate the world, but they can also overwhelm him and lead to their own evolution. The risk exists because projections make man a stranger to his own actions; they also elude him, because they are part of a *memetic ecology*. Consciousness and, to a certain extent, intelligence, depend on a complex informational network in which human and biological entities on the one hand, and technical and memetic entities on the other, interact. I'm not intelligent on my own, naked from the sky. I have a consciousness and a tiny intelligence because I'm a member of a human group, I have a language and a whole heritage of methods, brain maps, memes and intellectual technologies. I am but a tiny actor in a memetic ecology that encompasses, nourishes and constrains me, and which, in turn, I nourish in my own way, by projecting myself. *I think, therefore I am, in a network* in which neurons, human cognitive maps, languages, writing systems, books, computers, techniques, institutions, rules, customs, beliefs, superstitions, fashions and myths all interconnect, transform and shape my ecology. Gilles Deleuze and Félix Guattari spoke of "rhizomes[182]" that spread out, transgressing all classifications and connecting heterogeneous strata of being. Ilya Prigogine has shown that there is no radical break between the physical universe, with its laws and immobility, and the teeming world of imagination and inventiveness of the living, because within matter itself, we now also discover information, instability, sensitivity and bifurcations[183]. In the networks of memetic ecology, there is no distinction between thinking subjects, inanimate objects and ideas. All have a "soul", as the poet put it, all have a spirit, which contributes to shaping and informing the environment in which they evolve. For the techniques and memes that people have invented and projected are players in their own right, just like human beings, in a plastic collective that is constantly being redefined, which is culture and civilization. Without

---

182. Deleuze (Gilles) & Guattari (Félix), *Mille Plateaux (Capitalisme et schizophrénie, tome 2)*, Éditions de Minuit, 1980.
183. Prigogine (Ilya) & Stengers (Isabelle), *Between Time and Eternity*, Fayard, 1988.

writing, there would have been no universalist religions. Without Gutenberg, the emergence of modern science in the 16th and 17th centuries would probably not have taken place. Religions and science are closely dependent, for their propagation and replication, on the intellectual technologies that men project. The Reformation would have been unthinkable without the invention of the printing press, which multiplied the number of vernacular versions of Bibles. Public opinion and democracy would be mere dreams without the power of the press and books. It's important to understand that the ecology we're talking about is a self-organizing cognitive collective, not just made up of human beings[184]. Techniques and ideas play an essential role, constantly unbalancing, composing and recomposing the ecological environment in which these cosmopolitan entities - biological, technological, intelligent, hybrid - co-evolve.

Agriculture is certainly a fascinating example of how man's projections generate massive, profound and rapid metamorphoses of his memetic ecology. It was introduced some ten thousand years ago. Before then, human life was still governed by hunting and gathering. Humans didn't produce the food they needed; they had to understand nature in order to draw what it had to offer. This way of life was extraordinarily stable, based on small human societies bound together by sacred bonds and respect for tradition. The weight of the sacred and the taboo, which I've already mentioned, certainly helped to inhibit any innovation that might compromise the group's organization. But this rigidity was combined with an extraordinary adaptability to environmental conditions. The man of this era was capable of adapting to any terrain, from the polar cold to the scorching savannah, from tropical forests to swamps and deserts. Sensitive to all the ecosystem's messages, man had developed sensory, intuitive

---

184. Cf. Lévy (Pierre), *Les Technologies de l'intelligence*, La Découverte, 1990.

and manual abilities - relatively considerable in the grand scheme of things - that contemporary humans simply no longer possess. His society was coherent with its ecology, free of major internal contradictions, and thus escaped the destructive and violent impulses that would only come later.

These first human societies had a very slow population growth. If we go back a hundred thousand years or so, we think that the overall human population, concentrated mainly in Africa, was in the order of ten to one hundred thousand individuals - a very small number compared with today, but sufficient to ensure that a species was not in danger of extinction. Gradually, these societies multiplied and began to cover an immense part of the globe. This is what specialists call "the great expansion", which they date back to around 30 or 40,000 years ago, at a time when the human species may have reached a density close to saturation[185]. Demographic pressure led to emigration to Europe, America, Australia and other parts of the world. By the end of this expansion, it is estimated that the human population must have increased at least fivefold. Driven by demographic pressure, man's inventiveness and powers of projection increased tenfold. Primitive means of navigation had to be created from scratch to reach South Asia and then Australia from Africa, at a time more than 50,000 years ago. This technical inventiveness probably required the progress of language, which developed prodigiously and diversified into a multitude of languages spoken on every continent; these languages in turn enabling better adaptation, propagation and use of innovations. A new era could then begin: the Neolithic. It corresponds to the emergence of agriculture, and dates back some 10,000 years. This human projection did not fall from the sky like some kind of sudden illumination; the ancient societies of the Palaeolithic already possessed within them

---

185. *Cf.* CAVALLI-SFORZA (Luca), *Gènes, peuples et langues, op. cit.*

the virtualities of their own surpassing[186]. Hunting paved the way for animal husbandry, while knowledge of plants, seeds and tubers paved the way for agriculture. It's not impossible that rudimentary forms of animal domestication and cultivation may have developed before the Neolithic, but demographic pressure was insufficient to systematize and considerably amplify their extension. It was the demographic expansion of the species across the entire planet that led to an inevitable phenomenon: the concentration of populations in certain areas endowed with a favorable ecosystem, offering fertile land and suitable climatic conditions. Luca Cavalli-Sforza estimates that the Neolithic period certainly began in the Middle East[187] and lasted four to five thousand years, until the appearance of metals. Both agriculture and animal husbandry were quite diversified, involving a variety of species. Expansion was extremely slow, steady and inexorable. Thanks to radiocarbon dating, we know that wheat cultivation, for example, began in the Middle East and Anatolia around 9,500 years ago. It took three and a half thousand years, at an average speed of 1 km/ year, to reach England, after having spread throughout Europe[188]. Agriculture was born of demographic pressure; it will develop through memetic pressure.

There's no doubt that the increase in food supplies made possible by agriculture stimulated demographic growth and led to the expansion of new populations into new territories. Some of these territories, already occupied by certain human groups, may well have required the use of force to appropriate them. But these factors are not essential to understanding the rise of agriculture. The main factor is memetic and cultural. Imagine the arrival of new farmers, proudly endowed with their innovation, in a region still populated by hunter-gatherers.

---

186. *Cf.* MORIN (Edgar), *Le Paradigme perdu: la nature humaine, op. cit.*
187. And probably at around the same time, in China and Mexico.
188. CAVALLI-SFORZA (Luca), *Gènes, peuples et langues, op. cit.*

They live at low density, reproducing slowly at the rate of one child every four years. They are semi-nomadic, which means that when they travel, they have to carry everything they own with them, especially children under the age of three, whom they have to carry in their arms. The projection of the idea of agriculture in these men's brains is bound to sedentarize them, fixing them to a land they will no longer need to leave to find food. From then on, the process of imitation begins, and everything changes. We can have children more often, we can eat more easily, and in particular with milk, such a high-protein food, which is now at our fingertips. This was not possible before, not just for supply reasons, but for genetic reasons. All mammals, including humans, lose the ability to digest lactose after infancy. This sweet molecule is still harmful today in many adult humans[189]. Biologist Lynn Margulis explains[190] that a biological mutation spread among the populations of northern Mesopotamia around 8,000 years ago. The arrival of these mutant adults, who tolerated milk because they were better supplied with lactase, the enzyme that digests it, caused a revolution. By spreading genetically through ever larger populations, this lactose tolerance enabled humans to acquire animal proteins without having to kill their prey, and gave them new essential nutritional products such as yoghurt, butter and cheese. Better endowed with vitamin D, which is the vehicle for calcium, these humans suffered less from rickets or brittle bones.

These changes in lifestyle are considerable and have an immediate impact on demographics, which then increase by multiplication factors ranging from ten to a thousand. This is an exemplary case in which genetic and memetic factors are inextricably linked, while at the same time the projection of human ideas shapes an unprece-

---

189. This harmfulness is characteristic of populations that practiced dairy farming later, as is the case in Latin America in particular.
190. Margulis (Lynn) & Sagan (Dorion), *L'Univers bactériel, op. cit.*

dented memetic ecology. Sedentarization settles populations that have become agriculturalists into larger, more structured forms of organization: villages and towns. In this new environment, a whirlwind of new ideas will emerge, be exchanged and become fixed; some of them, subject to memetic selection, will disappear, while others will make a long journey through human evolution. It's not impossible, moreover, that it was at this first stage of sedentarization that warfare appeared: men, losing the hunting function that had devolved upon them in the family organization, were unlikely to lend themselves willingly to the less "active" work of breeding and cultivating plants, reserved more for women. What's more, owning land necessarily implied defending it, and gave rise to the desire to own more and more of it. Weapons for hunting will not be put away. They will be preserved and will evolve without limits, directed not only at game, but at other men. This is another long story.

A profound metamorphosis of human organization is thus taking place. The aggregation of human communities in the same place is combined with the emergence of new relationships that carry with them the seeds of an organization in which power, hierarchy and processes of defense against external threats are put in place. This is how the city came into being, through the natural aggregation of communities, but also through the conquest and regrouping of tribal, clan or village microstructures. It is here that a universe of life takes shape, with its center of power, its ritual sites, its granaries, its strongholds, its shops and its dwellings. As soon as the city appeared, the rudiments of the state were formed, administration branched out and religion took off. The division of labor necessarily appeared in this more complex structure, with the proliferation of trades and the establishment of outward-looking commercial relationships, first with surrounding villages, then with more distant lands. The mutation taking place is not unlike that of single-celled organisms which, through a long evolutionary process, were transformed by endosymbiosis into multi-cellular organisms practicing the division of labor. The mechanism is the same for both, propelled by the fundamental influence of the environment.

From the moment of his birth, man thus receives a double inheritance: genetic and memetic. What's important to understand is that memetic inheritance - the inheritance of culture, ideas and knowledge - is not superimposed on genetic heredity. Rather, it combines with it, creating stimuli or inhibitions that shape each individual, just as a phenotype is conditioned by genes. Edgar Morin expresses this characteristic very well: "Each culture, through its early *imprintings*, its taboos, its imperatives, its education system, its diet, the talents it requires for its practices, its behavioral modules in the ecosystem, in society, between individuals, etc., It represses, inhibits, favors, overdetermines the actualization of this or that aptitude, of this or that psycho-affective trait, puts multiform pressures on the whole of cerebral functioning, even exerts endocrine effects of its own, and, in this way, intervenes to co-organize and control the whole of the personality[191]." Memes do not supplant genes; it is their replication in the brain of an individual forming part of a particular society that complements genetic heredity, ensuring the perpetuation and evolution of human society. But I explained a moment ago that this replication does not mean the acrobatic leap of a meme from brain to brain. It's a reconstruction by the individual, a permanent *self-production* of the cultural system projected in each brain, and not just a single *reproduction of* the cultural system, from individual to individual, as we might have thought[192]. The human brain becomes the epicenter around which the information of all social, cultural, ecosystemic, memetic and technical activity

---

191. MORIN (Edgar), *Le Paradigme perdu, op. cit.*
192. Cf. BOURDIEU (Pierre) & PASSERON (Jean-Claude), *La Reproduction*, Éditions de Minuit, 1970.

unfolds. The brain must therefore not be conceived as a simple biological structure of unprecedented complexity; it must be understood as a component in its own right of *a larger*, all-encompassing *structure*, in permanent co-evolution and self-organization, which I invite you to discover in a few pages.

Technology is a component of this all-encompassing structure. It is, first and foremost, the memetic product of man's projected brain. To better understand what I mean by this, it's time, at this stage of our story, to go back to the definition of the meme and expand on it. A meme is a unit of cultural information - in a general sense, an "idea" - that replicates itself from brain to brain in the ways we've described. The meme resides in the human brain, but also in all the artificial extensions of the brain, invented by man to complete and extend his memory, such as books, computers and the most varied media of information. Whatever the form of storage, the meme always remains a meme. Whether stored in a human brain or in any other physical structure, the meme undergoes an evolutionary algorithm. This means that the structure of a meme can vary from brain to brain, in the sense that the cognitive maps of one individual are necessarily different from those of another. The meme, remember, behaves like an "instigator" triggering meaning. Are a fork, a bridge or a car a meme? These technical objects are totally related to memes, but they have a special nature. Like genes, memes produce phenotypes, i.e. observable representations. For Daniel Dennett, the meme is internal (but not necessarily confined to the human brain), while the design it shows to the world, "its way of affecting things in its environment[193]", is its phenotype. The phenotype is the instrument of human projection. It is the vehicle of the meme. Books, buildings and tools are meme *vehicles*. The humble wheelbarrow I use in my garden is the vehicle of a brilliant idea, a particularly well-replicated meme: the spoke wheel.

---

193. DENNETT (Daniel), *Is Darwin dangerous?*, Odile Jacob, 2000.

For a long time, technology held little interest for thinkers and philosophers, and some simply didn't take it seriously. As far back as the Greeks, its only recognized virtue was its ability to extend the work of nature by revealing its possibilities. Contemporary thinkers, when they evoke technology, are driven by two contradictory sentiments: one is to be ecstatic about its prodigies, the other is to fear its apocalyptic effects. But the vast majority refuse to consider it as anything other than an extension of science, a far nobler subject of study than vulgar technology. Traditionally, technology has been viewed from a naturalistic angle: a tool is an extension of a human organ. Anthropologist André Leroi-Gourhan is at the source of a "biological philosophy of technology" that places techniques within a naturalistic framework whose evolution is relatively predictable[194]. Technique would only exceptionally result from the reasons of science, and would fulfill primarily utilitarian functions. According to this perspective, technology exists only as an element of human culture[195], subject to human ends. This view is common sense. The discourse on technology is typically marked by human omnipresence: man is the measure of all things and the ruler of so many technical marvels, the fruit of his ingenious brain. Jacques Ellul points out that the "gigantic din of technology exploding in all directions[196]" is something we all think man intended. Did we walk on the Moon? It's the dream of mankind from the very beginning, finally realized. Every technical advance is the fruit of a human will that goes back to the earliest times. Ever since Icarus, man has wanted to fly: thanks to technology, he can do so today. Man's freedom grows with each technical advance. Is this really so? At a time when the "technosciences" are making their appearance in our world, with their trail of questions about mastering

---

194. Cf. LEROI-GOURHAN (André), *Milieu et techniques*, Albin Michel, 1945.
195. Cf. MUMFORD (Lewis), *Technique and Civilization*, Seuil, 1950.
196. ELLUL (Jacques), *Le Bluff technologique*, Hachette, 1988.

their power, when the computerization of society is becoming total, when the life sciences are capable of changing man, we are beginning to detect another nature of technology: that of empowerment and the split with human nature. "Technique is a contestation of man's natural condition: it is the obscure effort to push the human essence out of its hounds and its limits, and to project it towards an elsewhere that would no longer be either man's or nature's[197]." According to Jacques Ellul, technology has become independent of the human cultural milieu. He writes: "Technology has become autonomous, forming a devouring world that obeys its own laws, disavowing all tradition[198]". Heidegger denounces the "immeasurable monstrosity" of technology[199]. The philosopher Günther Anders, long unknown in France, was a disciple of Heidegger, friend of Hans Jonas and first husband of Hannah Arendt. As early as 1956, in his book *L'Obsolescence de l'homme (The Obsolescence of Man)* and some twenty years later, in *Nous, fils d'Eichmann (We, the Sons of Eichmann)*, he evoked the implacable evolution of technology: "Since the raison d'être of machines lies in performance, and even in maximum performance, they all need environments that guarantee this maximum. And what they need, they conquer. Every machine is expansionist, not to say "imperialist", each creating its own colonial empire of services... The original machine thus expands, becoming a "megamachine"... It creates this "colonial empire" for itself, and assimilates it to such an extent that it in turn becomes a machine - in short, there is no limit to self-expansion; the thirst of machines is unquenchable[200]."

---

197. BRUN (Jean), *Les Masques du désir*, Buchet Chastel, 1994.
198. ELLUL (Jacques), *La Technique ou l'Enjeu du siècle*, Economica, 2nd ed. 1999.
199. *Cf.* MILLET (Jean-Philippe), *L'Absolu technique: Heidegger et la question de la technique*, Kimé, 2000.
200. ANDERS (Günther), *Nous, fils d'Eichmann*, Payot & Rivages, 2003 - Cf. also *L'Obsolescence de l'homme*, Éditions de l'encyclopédie des nuisances & Éditions Ivrea, 2002.

Has technology, the product of human memetic activity, really become so autonomous as to impose itself on human societies with the force of blind destiny? Should we share the catastrophist visions of Ellul, Hottois[201], Heidegger and many others? Should we consider technology as an independent force, outside time, mankind and society? The memetic point of view leads us to consider the question differently. There is no clear-cut distinction between man and technology, any more than there is between life and science. It's always possible to introduce distinctions to facilitate analysis, but we mustn't take the operative concepts we forge for specific purposes to be radically separate realities. If we place things and techniques on one side, and people, languages, cultures and values on the other, radically separating them, then thinking starts to go off the rails[202]. Technology does not advance, alone, in full and strange autonomy, towards a grandiose goal, towards the "progress of mankind" or towards the "general improvement of mankind[203]". Technology is of memetic origin; it therefore develops in an authentically Darwinian perspective. Every invention borrows from the past and improves on it in small steps, some of which may prove revolutionary: the digital camera would not have been possible without the precedent of the film camera, the plastic bucket would never have seen the light of day if the iron bucket had never existed, and so on. All inventions are the fruit of an evolutionary process; they all climb, as Dawkins puts it, their own Mount Improbable. There is progress, but it is always towards something more specialized, more structured, more improbable. There is technological progress, but it is not inevitable. Technologies develop in lineages over time, just as animal species do. So where does this impression of empowerment and spontaneous

---

201. Cf. Hottois (Gilbert), *Le Signe et la Technique*, Aubier, 1984.
202. *Cf.* Lévy (Pierre), *Les Technologies de l'intelligence, op. cit.*
203. Basalla (Georges), *The Evolution of Technology*, Cambridge University Press, 1989.

development of technology towards mysterious and not always friendly goals come from?

The answer lies in the fact that we sometimes tend to forget that everything fits together. That man, his projections, his books, his ideas, his culture, his institutions, his techniques, are the linked and interconnected components of an all-encompassing whole in which human consciousness lies at the epicenter. Philosopher Karl Popper imagined this whole to be made up of three intertwined worlds, perfectly separate yet interdependent[204]. The three worlds are established as a cosmology, encompassing all forms of existence and experience. Popper first distinguishes World 1: this is the world of things and material states. It includes, on the one hand, inorganic objects (such as matter and energies), on the other, living biological organisms: plants, animals, the human body, and finally manufactured objects: the material projections of human creativity, tools, machines, books, works of art, music, and so on. World 2 is the world of states of consciousness, encompassing subjective knowledge and diverse experiences (perception, thought, emotions, intentions, memories, dreams, creative imagination). World 3 is the world of objective knowledge. It comprises, on the one hand, our cultural heritage encoded on material, philosophical, theological, scientific, historical, literary, artistic and technological substrates and, on the other, theoretical systems developed by man (scientific problems, critical arguments)[205]. World 3 is the specifically human world, corresponding to human civilizations. This is the world that contains memes. The three worlds are intimately interconnected by intense informational links. So, for example, our thinking, which belongs to

---

204. Cf. POPPER (Karl R.), *L'Univers irrésolu, plaidoyer pour l'indéterminisme*, Hermann, 1984 and POPPER (Karl R.) & ECCLES (John C.), *The Self and Its Brain*, New York, Springer-Verlag International, 1977.
205. Note that each of these entries can be expanded: for example, the "artistic" substrate covers all the plastic arts, crafts, architecture, music and so on.

World 2, depends in part on the autonomous problems and objective truths of theorems belonging to World 3. World 2 creates World 3, but World 2 is also partly created by World 3, in a feedback process. All three worlds are subject to evolutionary processes. The development of World 3 was very slow during the first tens of thousands of years of *Homo sapiens*. It was probably only when primordial human needs - food, shelter, security - were met that man began to participate fully in enriching World 3. At first, intellectual ideas from World 3, such as history or mythologies, were preserved in human memory. When writing came along, it was possible to codify all the ideas, knowledge and memes of the third world onto ever more numerous media, accumulated in World 1. Popper's three worlds provide a clear definition of the human process of knowledge. If this sounds abstract, let's take a concrete example. You are reading this book; you have in your hands a material reality, an object of paper and ink, which belongs to World 1. As you read, feelings will arise in you; these feelings belong to World 2. The book you are reading is a real object, as are the feelings you are experiencing, which are also real; these feelings are not pure, timeless virtualities. They are conditioned by the knowledge you have acquired in World 3. It is World 3 that will enable you to exercise your critical faculties, to identify the theories presented in this book, to confront them with your own presuppositions and, if necessary, to modify them. Our subjective knowledge is therefore strongly influenced by World 3.

This is possible because World 3 is partially autonomous. Let's look at this singular characteristic for a moment. If we take up Popper's cosmology, World 2 is where we perceive the realities of World 1, i.e., for example, nature or the surrounding environment. World 2 is where you can see a sunset, because it's in World 2 that individual sentient reality takes shape. All animals live in World 2. But you know very well that when you admire a sunset, you're not "stupidly" passive. Ideas come to mind, thoughts, neural maps light up. As we saw a few pages ago. Ideas and theories are not confined to a pre-existing, transcendent, immutable and eternal Platonic universe. They are not on the other side of the cave. They are situated on the plane of man's immanence; the third world is projected into the brains of men in the slightest of their acts and states of consciousness. What's important to remember is that this third world is created by man. This does not mean, however, that it does not possess a certain autonomy. So, for example, people create and produce theories which, if we can put it that way, are stored in World 3. But once created, these theories will live their own lives, enriching themselves in ways that the man who invented them never imagined. Popper cites the case of mathematics. The discoveries we make in this field are already contained in mathematical principles produced a long time ago. The discovery of integers, for example, is not a discovery in the strict sense of the term, since integers are a property contained in the logical axioms laid down by Euclid. But Euclid could never have suspected the existence of integers, which would not appear until several centuries later. The same applies to all human intellectual creations, from quantum mechanics and neuroscience to the information theories we use every day. Ideas, theories and memes, once projected by human beings, acquire their autonomy as soon as they enter World 3 and begin a process of endless expansion and enrichment, overturning previous theories until they replace them. But their expansion doesn't stop there, as these ideas influence our states of consciousness in World 2, our way of seeing things and apprehending reality. This phenomenon is exploding with the emergence of modern techno-scientific and informational theories, which not only retroact on World 2, but also have direct effects on World 1, notably the biosphere.

This growing empowerment is a legitimate concern for thinkers, who are reduced to admitting that no knowledge, no idea, no technology can claim to be innocent, harmless and without unforeseen effects. Any act of projection of human consciousness is a potentially productive act of predation, survival or utopia. Every human idea, every emitted meme, whether in the form of a work of art, a technique, a philosophy or a book, is inexorably subject to the law of natural selection; the fittest will win the privileges of replication, imitation, expansion and empowerment. Indeed, ideas are constantly engaged in an incessant struggle for survival and perpetuity, "they are living entities, cooperating, competing, trading and warring, influencing each other, devouring each other, breaking up, reforming, plundering and raping each other, in a tangle of increasingly interwoven relationships, in a state of *permanent sampling*, encoding-decoding-surcoding-hypercoding, deconstructing-reconstructing old forms, old machines, within new syntheses[206]." New information technologies take on a particular consistency in Popper's world of nested interfaces. The simple transmission of information described by classical theory is no longer sufficient to understand the innumerable interactions that take place between physical reality, sensible reality and the world of ideas; interactions immense in number, form and diversity, which come together at a nodal point of interconnection: the human brain. That's why I'd like to introduce the concept of hyperinformation.

---

206. DANTEC (Maurice G.), *Millenium Machines*, 1998 (text online at mauricedantec.com).

Interlude VIII

The decorator bird

In nature, man is not the only being capable of projection. There's another: the cradled bird. Nineteenth-century naturalists thought that mammals could be divided into two groups: humans and all other mammals. Similarly, birds fell into two categories: cradled birds and all other birds[207]. Which goes to show how singular his behavior was deemed to be. This distinction is well-deserved, as the cradled bird is the only animal to have given form to projections of itself.

This relatively common passerine lives in the forests of Australia and New Guinea. What's so extraordinary about it? It builds a cradle-shaped nest to attract and seduce the female. So far, you might say, this doesn't sound like very extraordinary information. But this cradle is very special. Imagine an aisle 60 cm long and 45 cm high. The male, an eminent builder, begins his work with a platform of intertwined branches, about 10 cm thick, into which he plants twigs of equal diameter and length, to build two parallel walls framing an open aisle at each end. Each wall requires several hundred twigs, and the whole arbour comprises almost seven thousand. It's quite an elaborate construction, you'll admit. But there's more. We've only just begun.

---

207. HALL (Edward T.), *Beyond Culture, op. cit.*

Our friendly bird, certainly considering that this construction is not pretty enough, decides to *decorate* it. To this end, in the same way that my wife goes shopping, he brings home a bewildering array of objects: white snail shells, iridescent insect carapaces, multicolored seeds, original pebbles, bone fragments, pieces of glass, clay or coal balls, aluminum pins, soda capsules, and even freshly picked flowers. In this way, he accumulates between five and twelve thousand objects representing around ten kilos of material, which is considerable for his size. Some varieties even paint the walls of their cribs: they smear the walls of their arbors with a coating made from berries mixed with a little saliva, producing a beautiful blue color.

This cradle - with its decoration - is not just an extension of a once brilliant plumage. It's also an object of display. It serves to attract a female. But this lady sparrow seems to be very capricious. She makes three visits to the cradle before making up her mind. The first time, she visits it alone, to form an opinion, and the second time, in the company of our decorator bird, who must be very proud to present his work. After careful consideration, the female decides on her partner. She then enters the cradle for a third time, and watches in delight as the male performs a complex mating dance in which he stiffens his legs, opens his wings, whistles and ahans sounds that can imitate galloping horses, barking dogs and other forest birds.

Immediately after mating, the flighty female flies off to a nearby wood and builds a simple nest in which to lay her eggs, leaving our decorator bird in her beautiful empty home.

9. Hyperinformation

With the emergence of the digital, the virtual and electronic networks, the concept of information has radically changed in nature. It is taking on unprecedented dimensions and producing anthropological consequences, some of which are still indiscernible. The metamorphosis of information into *hyperinformation* implies a different way of seeing, of becoming aware of reality, of grasping the universe. It reveals the complexity of our consciousness and the epicentral place of the human brain in the world - that of the planet, civilizations, cultures and all human projections. Apparently, everyone understands the meaning of the concept of information; in reality, it's complex and multiform, as difficult to define as that of being, matter or energy. It can be applied to anything - including being, matter or energy - but, unlike these three concepts, it does not designate an isolated reality. Information is essentially qualitative; it cannot be apprehended outside a universe that gives it meaning, since it is above all part of a *relationship*. It is perception of the outside world, exchange, adaptation, coordination and regulation with its environment. Information is organic. This means that the elements of which it is composed remain distinct; they are not confused, as chemical elements in fusion lose their heterogeneity. This character is fundamental, as it induces the *discontinuity of* information. As Bergson wrote: "Intelligence clearly represents only the discontinuous[208]". The discontinuous nature of information is fundamental today. It confers on information the possibility of choice, of distinction, of bifurcation between several mutually exclusive options. The discontinuity of information is an essential characteristic because, if we manage to transmute a continuous natural signal into a discontinuous one, we open up an immense field, that of *reproducibility*. All this may seem quite abstract to you, but you use these particularities of information in your daily life, particularly when you listen to music on your MP3 player or simply on a CD. You know that natural sound is a continuous sinusoidal signal, a propagating wave. If you can break down this continuous signal into independent units like a sequence of 0s and 1s, then you've done the work of a true alchemist. You have *transmuted*, not lead into gold, but the original sound into a sequence of binary codes. This "digitized" information can then be compressed, transmitted, reproduced completely identically and interpreted by a suitable "digital" player. This binary digitization has proved to be totally universal, extending to all fields: sound, images, text, data, biological codes. It has the ability to make "liquid[209]" what is solid; everything that can be digitized is translated into something else, digitized too. Matter, once made up of impenetrable heterogeneous substances, is now digitizable, i.e. "vaporizable" everywhere online. Digitization is interoperable, which means it can circulate between a multitude of digital receivers. Its logic is that of *convergence*. Boundaries between media are erased, differences in the nature of content substances become blurred, and broadcasting, communication and distribution systems are integrated into the same operational regime. Users, too, merge into a borderless globality that smoothes out all differences, be they linguistic or cultural.

---

208. BERGSON (Henri), *Essai sur les données immédiates de la conscience*, PUF, Coll. Quadrige, 2003.
209. KERCKHOVE (Derrick de), *L'Intelligence des réseaux*, Odile Jacob, 2000.

This technical metamorphosis, this transmutation, is the foundation of hyperinformation.

A *receiver is* needed not only so that information can be replicated, but also so that it can make sense. There is no such thing as information in itself, and it cannot be isolated from the system for which it makes sense. Information is not a simple concept: we can't say "it's a characteristic of such-and-such an object", because it's the receiver who constitutes it as such. Information is the link between transmission and reception, between sign and meaning, between consciousness and object, between instigator and meme; it is the hub of Popper's three worlds, which I mentioned in the previous chapter. Information is an internalization of the external universe, of a foreign world - be it that of nature or that of ideas - which can amaze or terrify us, reconstituted indirectly, progressively, through a succession of feedbacks and corrections. This duality implies that there is no immanent knowledge in the human brain; there is a veil that must be lifted[210], a separation that must be overcome. The world of information is a world populated by lures, truths and mirages, for it is a world left to our representation; the risk of illusion is part of the game.

The founding schemes of the fathers of information and communication research are, you will admit, outdated; they described a unidirectional process of transmission, whereas with hyperinformation, a multitude of adjustments emerge between "senders" and "receivers". The activity of communication must now be seen in an interactionist, dialectical representation, in which consumers of information appear as "producers of trajectories[211]" that are not necessarily coherent with the world in which they slip. The system for producing and distributing information is itself radically transformed; it is part of a logic of

---

210. Physicist Bernard d'Espagnat speaks of "veiled reality". Cf. *À la recherche du réel*, Gauthier-Villars, 1979.
211. Certeau (Michel de), *L'Invention du quotidien, I. Arts de faire*, Gallimard, 1990.

complexity and mutation that obeys its own rules of evolution. The interactivity between the individual's brain, the societal system and the hyperinformational system is total, consubstantial; a fusional and, certainly to a large extent, confusing whole emerges[212]. Karl Popper, in his analysis of the open society[213], believes that entry into the electronic age corresponds to the creation of a single global tribe, made possible by new structures of human interdependence characteristic of a post-literate world. Didn't Pierre Teilhard de Chardin emphasize that modern media constitute a global network - a "noosphere"[214] - enabling "the universal rise of the psyche".

The breakthrough of hyperinformational technologies in our societies has created a fracture zone over which we are trying to bridge the gap. For the first time in human history, we can process reality, matter and the objects we make, using codes, signals and memories associated with languages. Manipulations are less and less carried out by material processes and more and more by immaterial means. The ways in which more and more goods and services are exchanged between human beings are radically transformed. To expand, these technologies are being deployed in *networks*. Their nature is transforming structural relations of production, power and relations between users: the invention of cultural codes is now dependent on the technological capacities of individuals, groups and societies, and on their mastery of these technologies. The computer, hitherto regarded as an information-processing machine[215], is now seen as the linchpin of the hyperinformational society, because it is, in its relative and evolving sense, an extension of the human brain. Thus, for the first time in history, an individual can switch a signal directly to another individual

---

212. *Cf.* Ayache (Gérard), *La Grande Confusion, op. cit.*
213. Popper (Karl), *The Open Society and its Enemies*, Seuil, 1979.
214. Teilhard de Chardin (Pierre), *Le Phénomène humain*, Seuil, 1955.
215. The terms *calculator*, *computer* or *computer* are typical of this approach.

on the other side of the planet. Until now, this capability was reserved for national or transnational telecommunications organizations. This switched signal, enabling free passage across space in a fraction of a second, is identified by a process that has become instantly trivial: the *hyperlink*, which enables us to jump with a simple click from one network node to another, from one computer to another, from one piece of information to another, from one universe to another, from one brain to another. It drives the accelerated, chaotic evolution of the world's memetic ecology. It frees up access to information, once locked away like a treasure, infusing it everywhere, leaving traces of knowledge in its wake. It opens up access to a vast, fluid and ever-moving network of research centers, libraries, data banks, men and women, media and bookstores, all repositories of billions of available memes. Hypertext opens up the horizon of a tumultuous ocean, leaving individual navigators free to make their own choices, whether they are responsible for drowning in the memetic ocean or conquerors of the knowledge they seek. The interconnection of computers thus becomes a potential medium for collective intelligence[216] and the Web can be conceived as heralding and gradually realizing "the unification of all texts into a single hypertext, the fusion of all authors into a single collective, multiple and contradictory author", with a view to the emergence of a single memory, or even a single consciousness and, perhaps, a "global brain[217]". In a similar vein, Derrick de Kerckove points out that "hypertext transforms the memory of each individual into the memory of all", and considers the Web to be the "first global memory[218]".

We've now entered the world of *connectivity*. Screens and "intelligent objects" are invading our universe, and sources of information

---

216. Lévy (Pierre), *L'Intelligence collective*, La Découverte, 1997.
217. Bloom (Howard), *The Lucifer Principle. The Global Brain, op. cit.*
218. Kerckhove (Derrick de), *L'Intelligence des réseaux, op. cit.*

are multiplying in logarithmic proportions. The public voice is conquered by all those who want to take it over and echo, in the global echo chamber, a broken-down reality. The movement is irreversible and seems perfectly uncontrollable. This veritable memetic explosion, the creator of an expanding universe, is rapidly composing the new landscape of our daily environment. A landscape in permanent reorganization, which folds up here, explodes elsewhere, reconstitutes itself there, and propagates itself in all zones of space where the hyperinformational force moves. Its deployment is organic; it does not take place on a simple scale. Its complex, dynamic forms reproduce themselves on all scales, shifting unpredictably from one space to another within a living universe.

Ever since the advent of writing 5,000 years ago in Mesopotamia, knowledge has continued to spread. For a long time, writing was reserved for the sacred and secret. With the book, writing opened minds. The generations that followed Gutenberg were exposed to a growing variety of information, ideas, images and memes. Photography, cinema, radio and television were all moving in the same direction: to make the world more visible, more accessible, more transparent and open to free memetic circulation. Today, we're simply continuing the millennia-old movement towards transparency, which has now reached its apogee. Technologies allow us to observe everything we want to see, to know everything we want to know, to know everything we want to know. At any given moment, we can observe, live from space, images of a cyclone in the Atlantic Ocean. With the click of a mouse, we can access all the world's libraries and research centers. The sphere of potential knowledge is growing out of all proportion. We're looking at the construction site of a new Tower of Babel, erected from scattered, discordant and heterogeneous parcels of knowledge. In the world of hyperinformation, human communities and individuals interact according to the flows they produce. They are linked to each other by their multiple social, cultural and informational relations; they are also linked to the encompassing totality, which we defined in the previous chapter, by the same type of relations. But they are incapable of curbing the hyperinformational system's tendency towards autonomy. Located in World 3, if we take up Popper's cosmology, hyperinformation acquires its own dynamic and constitutes an autonomous process that tends to escape human control. In the world of hyperinformation, language no longer possesses only the memory conferred by writing, nor the capacity for automatic reproduction provided by printing, nor the near-ubiquity of audiovisual media. It *also* possesses the capacity for autonomous action. Because language, too, is projected into another entity, software, which is, strictly speaking, the language of the machine. A language adapted to computers and networks, capable of acting on its own, interacting with other software, creating combinations of signs of all kinds, triggering other machines and robots, and replicating itself even more widely than the printed word. Replication and growth at a speed never before seen in human history. Remember that the Web you now use on a daily basis only appeared in 1994. Before that date, less than 1% of the human population was connected to the Internet. Today, in less than twenty years, more than 1 billion people are connected worldwide. On the scale of cultural evolution, such rapid spread has never been seen before. It took generations for the cultural consequences of the printing press to be felt. Today, in less than a generation, the civilizational mutations caused by this acceleration in the empowerment of technical dynamics are perfectly unforeseeable.

This impression of the growing empowerment of technologies is all the stronger as the mechanism for replicating the memes conveyed by hyperinformational flows accelerates. You now know that a good method of replicating a meme is imitation. However, in the world of hyperinformation, the factors of memetic imitation are considerably multiplied by the exacerbation of a deep-seated impulse that the philosopher René Girard[219] has well described, and which he calls *mimetic desire*. By analyzing the great novels of Cervantes, Stendhal and Dostoyevsky, Girard detects a very particular mechanism of human desire: desire is not autonomously fixed along a linear trajectory [subject *k* object], but according to a triangular relationship [subject *k* model *k* object], in which the subject doesn't know *a priori* what he or she desires. If he encounters an individual who possesses something that he does not, and who seems to fill this individual with fulfillment - happiness, pleasure, social status, etc. - then the subject will be fascinated, not by the object possessed by the other, but by the fullness that the object confers on the other. The concept of mimetic desire - and this is what makes it so interesting - does not stop here. Indeed, mimetic desire is *circular*. René Girard shows that the model is not passive; it doesn't wait for any manifestation of imitation from the subject. On the contrary, it does everything in its power to provoke imitation. If the object he possesses were not desired by another, it would be of no interest. The object's value lies in the other's desire for it. The model will therefore always generate more competition, i.e. provoke the emergence of a rival, which it will then itself have to supplant. Thus begins the infernal circularity of mimetic desire. The more the model reinforces his desire for the object, the more the subject will notice; by detecting the other's intention, according to the "mirror neuron" mechanism I mentioned earlier, he will see confirmation of the object's importance and redouble his efforts to possess it. In this way, both subject and model contribute to the emergence of the other as a rival. If one of the two introduces a difference of any kind (changing the desired object), the imitation will continue despite this change, in a kind of infinite headlong rush. Mimetic desire is one of the driving forces behind hyperinformation. It plays

---

219. Cf. GIRARD (René), *Mensonge romantique et vérité romanesque*, Hachette Littérature, 1999.

to the full, without limit, since information can be reproduced ad infinitum, at the lowest possible cost. *The desired object becomes information itself.* This is the source of a veritable mimetic fever that never ceases to grow and run riot. It affects both producers and receivers of information, and is characterized by the widespread reproduction of information, creating a snowball effect and functioning as a kind of auto-intoxication[220].

This mechanism of large-scale replication of memes, whether informative, cultural or scientific, generates an extraordinary superabundance of information, but paradoxically also produces uniformity of thought and of the world around us. "All around us, we sense that the alibi of modernity serves to bend everything under the implacable level of sterile uniformity[221]." This reflection by Ignacio Ramonet reveals a fundamental contradiction in our societies. They are bending under the weight of abundance - particularly of information - but, at the same time, they are tending towards ever greater uniformity. They are developing under the banner of complexity, while at the same time being marked by simplicity and oversimplification. This contradiction in our societies reflects the contradiction between a homogenized, standardized, efficient reality and a multiple, complex reality, rich in the universality of human beings. Uniformity is the expression of this paradox; it proceeds by reducing the immense choice offered by the abundance of sources and information from reality. From then on, the world's colors are chosen from a single palette: the same cars, the same fashions, the same streets, the same traffic jams, the same restaurant chains, the same logos on office buildings, the same films, the same TV series, the same music... An expansive and triumphant *world culture.* The plethora of information then takes on the status

---

220. I developed this theme in *La Grande Confusion*, analyzing journalistic work in particular from this angle.
221. RAMONET (Ignacio), *Géopolitique du chaos*, Galilée, 1997.

of an "empty sign", with no real referent other than itself. By losing its meaning and its referent, information also loses its function as a *mimesis* of the world; it becomes a sounding board for internalized social discourse, revealing our collective modes of thought, collective opinion and dominant memes; it becomes *a machine for manufacturing stereotypes*.

In today's hyperinformational digital society, the stereotype appears as one of the most important modules for fixing and transporting information. It contributes to the construction and solidification - in Greek, *stereos* means solid - of identity and a sense of belonging. It feeds individual and collective memories, but also helps to shape them. The power of the stereotype lies in its *digitized* nature. In effect, it is a frozen form, the memetic "instigator" described by Robert Aunger. The stereotype is a concentrate of reality, sampled in such a way that it can fulfill two functions: on the one hand, its identical reproducibility, and on the other, its capacity to become a trigger of meaning in the cognitive consciousness of individuals. The stereotype acts as a particularly precise and effective vector of information to penetrate the brain. The stereotype calls up memory and is called up by it. In this sense, it is in the realm of *allegory*, which is a reminder of representations already known. Allegory activates a conjunction of symbols and connotations already present in the consciousness, activating the neural maps described by Edelman; indeed, this is its etymological meaning: *allos*, "other" and *agoreo*, "I speak". Umberto Eco explains its nature perfectly: "In its fireworks, it brings into play images already seen elsewhere [...] it is an immediate reminder of codes already known that comes into play. [Allegory refers to scenarios and intertextual frames with which we are already familiar[222]". It also refers to other allegories and stereotypes, with which it establishes systems

---

222. Eco (Umberto), *Semiotics and the Philosophy of Language*, PUF, 1992.

of neural relationships. In this way, stereotypes act as preconceived and fixed memetic modules, placed in interrelation. They determine our representation of reality, our ways of thinking, feeling and acting, in the socio-cultural context in which they are embedded. Whether they bear the stamp of a "burning topicality" or are absorbed into the generality of a global vision of the world, they are nonetheless part of the value system that circulates them. Stereotypes are the fundamental building blocks of collective thought, emerging at a given moment in its memetic ecosystem, with its own language and representations.

The universality and diversity of knowledge available today through hyperinformational flows call for a collectivization of knowledge. It is now impossible for a single human being or group to master all the knowledge made available on digital networks. The Encyclopedia used to mean a circle of knowledge, i.e. a linear, one-dimensional geometric figure, closed in on itself through an infinite number of recursions. Today, the possibilities offered by digitization and computerized modes of circulation and network navigation are creating a new type of knowledge organization. Just as printing profoundly transformed the practice of clerics and scholars, hyperinformation is generating a new knowledge revolution. We are no longer dealing with a one-dimensional circle of knowledge, or even a single hypertextual network; we are confronted with a multidimensional space made up of dynamic, interactive representations expressed through a multitude of discursive and non-discursive forms: still or moving images, sounds, texts, interactive simulations, databases, expert systems, virtual realities, animated cartographies. Pierre Mac Orlan invented the "passive adventurer", one who "without moving from his place, dreams and combines, like powerful cocktails, adventures[223]."

---

223. MAC ORLAN (Pierre), *Petit Manuel du parfait aventurier (1920)*, Mercure de France, 1998.

In the 1920s, his contemporary Paul Morand proposed a surprisingly contemporary, complex, fragmented and kaleidoscopic vision of the world in his collection *Rien que la Terre*[224]. His panoptic gaze privileges space over history, surface over depth. What emerges is an accelerated impressionism, close to the nature of today's information flow. Morand invented an aesthetic of the coq-à-l'âne and the *shaker*; today, we would say an aesthetic of hypertext and *zapping*. He invented a new relationship between universality and diversity, where beauty is in the mixed, where totality is complexity, juxtaposition, mosaic.

The complex nature of this kaleidoscopic universe brings us closer to the complexity of the world than it distances us from it. Instead of the rigid organization of knowledge into disciplines, or the chaotic fragmentation of data, the new informational space dematerializes separations and offers a dynamic cartography in constant metamorphosis. Passive reception gives way to active experimentation. Each consultation, each inscription in this space, shapes it; each unanswered question or interrogation puts it in tension and signals the zones that call for invention. Links and contexts, references and openings weave a self-explanatory mesh. There's no need for speeches, comments or justifications; the way in which a new proposition relates to another doesn't have to be explained. It's what I call *meta-information*. In this space, information is called up, ordered, distanced, brought together, grouped, contracted, juxtaposed... it revolves around the individual; he or she is no longer a simple, unassuming receiver who receives information. It inverts the traditional pattern of communication, placing itself at the very *center of* the informational whirlwind. Meta-information actualizes another configuration of truth: that of the multitude of possible points of view. In this way, it brings individual trajectories into a collective space. Human brains infuse the signs they perceive into another space they know or know to exist. They

---

224. MORAND (Paul), *Rien que la Terre (1925)*, Grasset, 2000.

establish a depth of meaning between spaces. Information consumers move from one informational space to another space of meaning; there is permeability between spaces and fluidity of complementary relationships. In the meta-information system, individuals transhume from one space to another, forging their consciousness of things on a set of hypotheses, probabilities and values, and no longer just on a selection of information disseminated by those who had the exclusive privilege of possessing it.

Hyperinformation is overturning the nature of our relationship with the world, transforming the way we represent it and act upon it, and changing our social skin. Its scale is that of the planet, as well as that of the human brain itself, an entangled stakeholder in a flow that both drives and is driven by it. Its space-time is both the universe and man's neural abyss. This force is not regulated, it is not controlled; *it is*. Its destiny is expansion and universality; it is irreducible. It draws the new moving maps of knowledge, truth and falsehood, on which *terrae incognitae* appear and disappear, only to reappear again, elsewhere. It is a driving force, a force of mutation whose energy spreads to all strata of our societies, forging a new human condition.

Interlude IX

When the media tremble

Traditionally, the journalist is a reducer of complexity; this is his function as a popularizer, a transmitter of information and knowledge. This noble function is what gives journalists their very special status in our Western world. They enjoy privileges and base their identity on concepts that have the force of myth and the sacred: objectivity, independence, freedom of conscience, Truth, Democracy, and so on. These myths forge the identity and functional closure of this profession.

The traditional form of media sets boundaries on the path to reality. The medium, whatever it may be, always places itself in an intermediary position - it's in its etymological nature - between the real and the viewer. Its function is to bring reality to the viewer. In this spirit, live broadcasts are designed to reduce the distance between them, to simulate an immediate reality (i.e., without a mediator). This media initiative to weld the real to the spectator as much as possible, to reduce the distance, is an impossible undertaking, because the direction of movement is always the same: from the real to the spectator.

When viewers themselves reverse the direction of media logic - in other words, when they decide to go towards reality, and no longer wait for it to be brought to them on a screen - then traditional media tremble and falter, as they lose all intermediary function, all media

167

status. This reversal of the media's meaning is based on the desire for *meta-information*, in the sense of seeking out bits and pieces of reality in another space, beyond the information itself. This desire for meta-information is based on a logic of action and an ethic of responsibility. It can be applied in a variety of ways, depending on the individual, his or her capacity, objectives and intentions. The desire for meta-information tends to become a horizon that concentrates and polymerizes all information practices. It thrives in the hyper-informational multitude, in the confusing prism it offers, but it is a possible path towards greater clarity and intelligence. By experimenting with different possible forms of hypothesis and probability, it is consistent with the complex mechanics of today's systems. The desire for meta-information does not deny uncertainties; on the contrary, it integrates them. It works with probabilities and uncertainties with the aim of providing knowledge and orientation in the chaotic universe of world representations.

How can journalists still play their role in this profound hyperinformational transformation, in which the receiver of information is placed in the middle of the information, free to make all his or her own choices and take all his or her own initiatives, including that of issuing the information himself or herself? Today's public no longer expects journalists to reduce the complexities of the world so that they can better understand it, for two reasons: 1) they no longer trust them; 2) they know that the world is now too complex for them to be satisfied with a single "angle of attack", a single interpretation or an artificially clear-cut, Manichean opinion. He demands exactly the opposite of the journalist. He asks them to help him present the full range of content, in all its diversity and contradiction, to show him the widest possible spectrum of interpretations. Journalists are no longer expected to simplify complexity, but rather to privilege complex points of view. This fundamental change in the role journalists are expected to play requires them to embark on a veritable professional revolution without delay.

10. The human condition

The cave paintings of Lascaux and Altamira reveal *Homo sapiens'* very first imaginary connection with the world. That's what makes them so moving. For the first time, the sign, the symbol, the figurative act, undertook to continuously represent to the mind the beings and things of the external world. A total imaginary representation, generated even in the absence of the objects represented. The world thus becomes invasive in the human brain. But, conversely, the mental representations and images germinating in the brain are projected outwards, invading the world in their turn. It is in this cross-relationship that the ideological and practical organization of the imaginary link with reality is constructed. There's nothing rational about this construction, as Descartes understood it, because the brain is chaos. It is the seat of Brownian movements, of intense quantum activity. Our cerebral activity has nothing in common with that of a computer, as I've said several times, because it works with fuzzy and uncertain data, manipulating them according to laws that are still random, often erroneous, sometimes (self)corrected. The brain, a hyper-complex organ-system, operates in the midst of informational noise, adapting to it[225] and also drawing from it the springs of its

---

225. "Order comes from noise" wrote Heinz von FOERSTER in *Principles of Self Organisation*, New York, Pergamon, 1962.

imagination, dreams and creativity. But this magnificent object has a flaw. The intense activity that characterizes it, at all times, even during the deepest sleep, is powerless to distinguish between what comes from outside and what comes from within. The human brain is not equipped to discern reality from hallucination, fantasy from reality, the subjective from the objective. None of the information coming from the outside carries with it the criteria to reduce this ambiguity. Only consciousness is capable of doing this, by activating environmental control models that validate external perceptions, on the one hand, and cortical control models involving memory and logical reasoning, on the other. The latter draw on the memetic fund of learning and culture to clear up ambiguities. But not all. Our minds are always full of illusions, fantasies, hallucinations and follies that endure beyond time, crystallizing in beliefs, superstitions, religions and hatreds. The brain constantly moves back and forth between its environment, its culture and its memory, to establish its truth or the solution to its uncertainties. Truth and solutions are always being called into question, and then further questioned. The brain is a gap that never closes, the seat of a never-ending struggle between *Homo sapiens* and *Homo demens*[226].

The eruption of hyperinformation into our universe accentuates the fracture that is part and parcel of the human spirit. Diverse experiences of reality, culture and the world now coexist, without being mutually exclusive, superimposed on one another. Traditional experimentation coexists with tensions in explosive phases of innovation. Argentine philosopher Nestor Garcia Canclini has developed the theory of "hybrid culture[227] " to describe this state, where old and new memes coexist and interpenetrate to such an extent that boundaries become increasingly blurred. The hyperinformational system thus produces

---

226. *Cf.* MORIN (Edgar), *Le Paradigme perdu, op. cit.*
227. CANCLINI (Nestor Garcia), *Culturas hibridas*, Ediciones Paidos Iberica, 2001.

a hybridization that can be reduced neither to the simple mixing of genres nor to new syncretisms based on the recomposition of traditional elements. Hybridization refers to the rupture caused by new representations of the world. It manifests itself in the recomposition of scattered, heterogeneous elements. The individual then calls on "oblique strategies" to navigate these forms of hybridization, transactions between heterogeneous or divergent meanings, revealing the unresolved conflicts that agitate his brain. What emerges from this conflicting hybridization is the impossibility of avoiding the memetic torrent produced by hyperinformational flows, an imaginary torrent that invests all the workings of society and leaves a deep imprint on the human imagination and its projections. Fiction and imagination, the virtual and the real, information and misinformation, all blend and combine in the same movement, in which reality is not represented, but expressed: *it plays on feeling*. All that remains is fantasy. The world is no longer looked at; it is doomed to immediate, almost obscene devouring. A hypervision in close-up, a dimension without hindsight, an unguarded promiscuity of the brain and sensitive reality.

Emotion is thus placed at the epicenter of events and individuals, giving new meaning to what happens to them, to what connects them. We've always known that emotions are part and parcel of human identity, consubstantial with human nature. For a long time, they represented the wild side of the human being, the side that society had to banish or at least channel. For the Ancients, Greek tragedy was a *catharsis*, a purgatory for the emotions. Emotion was considered evil, a poison, a "peccant mood[228]", which had to be purged. Sociologist and historian Norbert Elias[229] highlights how emotions have been blacklisted throughout the West since the end of the Middle Ages. He explains that the guiding principle of our civilization has been a

---

228. *Cf.* ARISTOTLE, *Poetics*.
229. Cf. ELIAS (Norbert), *The Dynamics of the West*, Calmann-Lévy, 1994.

relentless repression of affectivity, with the code of politeness constituting an essential cog in the mechanism for normalizing behavior. This ideal of rational man, conceptualized and widely popularized by Descartes, was to last for several centuries. Emotions were purely and simply passions to be banished[230]. Evolutionary theorists, following in Charles Darwin's footsteps, explained that animals and humans alike had acquired an emotional reaction capacity to defend themselves in the struggle for life, but that by the time we reached the *Homo sapiens* stage, this function was no longer useful and had even become a factor of handicap and maladjustment.

However, the American neurobiologist Antonio Damasio concluded his experiments by asserting that the ability to reason is rooted in our emotional being[231]. Reason and emotion are not antagonistic; emotion plays a major role in the development of rational decisions, indeed, it is the driving force behind them. However, we must be aware of this. Human beings differ from animals in that they are aware of their emotions. Possessing language and an evolved memory, humans metabolize their emotions, i.e. they are capable of integrating and internalizing them, in an attempt to master them. Once metabolized, an emotion becomes a feeling. In this way, we establish a causal relationship between the effects of the emotion on our body and what triggered it. The sentient being can remember different emotional episodes with their causes, he can foresee that a certain event is likely to provoke a certain emotion, and he situates his emotion in relation to an inter-individual and social environment. In this way, he escapes the tyranny of animal reflex

---

230. Until the 1960s and 1970s, all academic psychology took the reductionist view that emotions served no purpose and were therefore not worthy of in-depth study. Freudian psychoanalysis regards emotion as a secondary phenomenon, preferring affect. Laplanche and Pontalis's *Vocabulaire de la psychanalyse* simply ignores the word "emotion" [LAPLANCHE (Jean) & PONTALIS (Jean-Bertrand), *Vocabulaire de la psychanalyse*, PUF, 1998].
231. *Cf.* DAMASIO (Antonio), *L'Erreur de Descartes : la raison des émotions*, Odile Jacob, 1995 and *Le Sentiment même de soi*, Odile Jacob, 1999.

automatism and acquires a certain sense of right and wrong. That's the theory. But in practice, things are not so clear-cut.

Emotion is a short-lived, intense shock. It triggers a cascade of operations in our brain and can, through the phenomenon of contagion and meme epidemics, be capable of directly impacting the collective in an anarchic aggregative fusion. It is born in the very depths of ourselves, only to overtake us, leaping from brain to brain, from the individual to the social. This is how we explain the great movements of crowds, and compassionate or festive impulses. Emotional fever never lasts very long, but it leaves deep marks on human brains. What's more, when subjected to intense emotional demands, the human brain dulls its ability to properly metabolize emotions into feelings. Emotional over-saturation is the hallmark of contemporary society, which is exposed to intense flows of hyper-information. Overabundance of messages, multiplication of sources, *ad nauseam* repetition, strong, raw, direct images, in plasma and HD, omnipresent sounds, in stereo, *surround* sound, etc., form the emotional environment of today's humans, which is only a watered-down foretaste of the one that research laboratories are preparing for them tomorrow.

The disruption of the emotional metabolism process opens the door to new social practices, alien to our usual modes of representation. In our chaotic, complex world, the language we used to metabolize our emotions and represent reality is no longer sufficient. Our modes of representation, which form the intimate links between our imaginations and reality, are no longer unique, because the certainty of our representation of the world has been abolished. On the one hand, the certainty of reality is receding; on the other, it is metabolized into a fragmentation of multiple, hybridized representations, an accumulation of diffracting modes of representation. Society is gradually freeing itself from its fixed frames of representation, discovering new spaces and new realities. *Virtual* worlds are a resolute expression of this.

The emergence of hyperinformation, with its prodigious capacities for digitization and code manipulation, has produced something special and unprecedented in human history: it has given rise to hybrid entities, situated between what is real and what is not. Computers have turned the rules of representation on their head, creating an intermediate link between the object and the project; in so doing, they have liberated the virtual, hitherto the prisoner of mere imaginary activity. Seeing the virtual as proposed by computer engineering, particularly in the field of simulation, means completely redefining the notions of image, object and perceptual space. Our environment contains, sometimes unwittingly, the beginnings of this new virtual reality. A five-year-old child today can move a computer mouse; what he doesn't know is that, through this now ordinary gesture, he is virtually manipulating immaterial objects: texts, images, windows; he is operating on an artificial reality. The virtual creates a strange state where the image is no longer representation, but presentation; where it is no longer figure, but function. The effects of this situation are not confined to the primacy of the virtual over the real, of the image over the object, of the machine over man. The new redistribution of notions of object/image or real/virtual also concerns the constitution of digitally modeled virtual objects that are sensitive to their environment. These virtual objects - which include simulation tools - can be mechanical parts, landscapes, climatic phenomena or economic strategies. They act as *ideal* models of real objects. The virtual appears here as a new dimension of the real, not intended to replace it, but to envelop it with an extension, a layer of possibilities that are no longer imaginary: "a concrete thought[232]".

For as long as man has tried to represent reality, the model and its image have always been perfectly distinct categories. Miron carving the strength of *Discobolus* in marble. Brunelleschi at last discovered

---

232. WEISSBERG (Jean-Louis), "Réel et virtuel", in *Multitudes*, March 1992.

the secrets of perspective, the illusion of depth. From the princes of Baroque trompe-l'œil to those of modern hyperrealism, every artistic era has sought to excel in the art of simulacra, that is, in the art of breaking through reality and wresting it from the gravitational force of its representation. Today, with hyperinformation technologies, the virtual image dispenses with the interaction of light with a sensitive surface; it no longer needs the real, since it can be produced concretely, through abstract manipulations. These are mathematical representations that directly produce the visible. The image thus frees itself from the materiality of the world, constituting itself as a pure abstraction. Stripped of all materiality, it can be manipulated in the same way as ideas or language, without having to submit to the laws of matter or light. This is a true revolution. Freed from all materiality, the virtual becomes a world of its own, alongside the real world; the image leaves its support and becomes a place - a second life, a *Second Life* - where we can move around, meet other people, work, practice our hobbies, have emotions, live. The fusion of images with the real world forces us to discern what, in our view and knowledge, depends on reality and what depends on our image of it. Combining the real and the image, the virtual questions both on the question of belief, merging them in the same doubt.

Homo sapiens may well have reached that stage in his evolution where it's the objects he makes that look at him. Paul Klee said: "Now objects see me[233]". Perhaps the objects are questioning our propensity to be unable to cope with reality to any great extent, and to seek to escape it by recreating it. Man escapes reality, in mind and body too. Digital information, through languages, was external to man. With the virtual, man, in his body, has also become a medium of information. *Borrowed bodies* in the avatars of video games and virtual realities, *bodies augmented* by the addition of peripheral organs, *bodies*

---

233. Quoted in Paul Virilio, *La Machine de vision*, Galilée, 1988.

interactivated as biometric information platforms, *bodies* permanently *connected* physically and mentally to other bodies on the network. The road to *Homo sapiens 2.0* seems to have already been paved.

The emergence of hyperinformation is producing changes of an anthropological nature. In man's relationship with reality, it shatters the certainties that enabled us to construct our perceptions and consciousness. The interrelationship between Popper's World 1 and World 2 has been turned upside down. What's more, hyperinformation also has an impact on human temporality. In today's hyperinformational universe, time contracts to the instant, the dimension of the immediate present, opening up the gap through which reality passes, the past is diluted and new history is forged.

The hyperinformational society is the revelation and catalyst of a singular trend: the valorization of the *instant*, of "real time". The pursuit of real time means reducing waiting times for information to zero, reducing time to an extremely efficient but artificial pseudo-time. Indeed, real time short-circuits the natural time of exchanges, and collides with a cosmological and human reality. Real time is always on standby. It is an inflexible, mathematical time, clocked to the rhythm of processors, at several hundred million cycles per second. Real time doesn't beat to our rhythm; it has taken us out of time. Man possesses intelligence and thought that obey a slow rhythm when confronted with change; the machine, on the other hand, processes numbers and *bits* that offer no resistance to change. The linear time of human history is a time that doesn't chase time, it's a *slow* time. Real time, immobile and empty of substance, a bubble of new time, is the ideal of this world, its end and its reality. It is a retracted time that is no longer sequential, but superimposed on others, weightless, punctual and simultaneous, at the limit of possible acceleration: the speed of light. The collision of the[234] time wall creates an unprecedented event:

---

234. Virilio (Paul), *Cybermonde, la politique du pire*, Textuel, 1996.

history now unfolds in global time. Until now, history has unfolded in local times and spaces: those of countries, regions and nations. Local histories have been shaped by successive struggles for independence, the assertion of personalities, against universal time; this is what makes our histories so rich and tragic. Today, history unfolds in a universal time that is instantaneous. Real time takes precedence over real space, disqualifying distances in favor of infinitesimal duration.

You'll probably ask me why modern man is so absurdly caught up in instantaneous time. My answer is that the new hyperinformational systems have changed the physical nature of time. Our vision of time and duration is intuitively linear and one-dimensional. We tend to consider that evolutions, i.e. the paths taken by phenomena over time, are inscribed on extrapolable lines, drawn in an empty, perfect and pure universe, with no influence whatsoever from the systems that surround, shape and encompass them. But why shouldn't time change? Biologist Joël de Rosnay explains that time, "our standard of reference, could expand 'from within' or contract 'from without'. A new relativity could be born, enriched by the experience of biology and the information sciences.[235]" There would thus be a relationship between time and information; the passage of time could be linked to the production of information. To justify this idea, de Rosnay sees information as potential time, as a "reserve of time". The more potential time we create, the more we indirectly compensate for the flow of universal time. In biology, for example, the information contained in genes produces potential time: evolutionary mechanisms save the obligatory passages - experiments and mutations - already inscribed in genes. In the field of information and culture, the process is identical. The accumulation of memes constitutes a "time capital" that can be used today and by future generations. What is a library or a museum if not also a reserve of humanity's potential time-capital? The accu-

---

235. Cf. Rosnay (Joël de), *L'Homme symbiotique*, Seuil, 1995.

mulation of instructions needed to perform a given gesture creates capital, which saves time and enables the task to be performed more efficiently and rapidly. It can then easily be replicated and propagated in the memetic environment. The first gestures were groping around, stumbling over errors, making corrections, then stabilizing into models. Subsequent generations, reproducing the model, gain time.

But what happens when original information and memes become plethoric and overabundant, as is the case in today's hyperinformational system? In this situation, new information increases memetic complexity and generates potential time; *it adds time to time*. To be more precise, it creates time within time. Information creates a time bubble of its own, representing the environment in which it evolves. The reservoir of memes is sufficiently dense, the accumulated time capital sufficiently large, to generate an impact on time. The temporal bubble created "curves" time, as if the memetic reservoir were made up of particles of time conferring a specific mass on the whole: "The creation of original information, the networking and parallelization of information, its memorization in data banks, 'curves' space-time by producing a pool, an attractor[236]." The Internet is a typical case of temporal densification: each user contributes memes, whether in the form of blogs, sites, comments, images or articles in community newspapers, and cumulatively reinvests the interest generated by the informational capital created at the outset. The many communities of open-source software developers are no different; they accumulate the experiences of members scattered across the network, creating a capital of information - of memetic "instructions" - from which everyone draws, and which everyone enriches. The temporal bubble thus created considerably alters the space-time of each member of the community. In the context of hyperinformational systems, in which a multitude of actors and complex systems produce and disseminate

------

236. *Ibid.*

information in parallel, we see a set of simultaneously evolving time bubbles forming ensembles, organized and hierarchized according to their temporal density. When a temporal bubble is dense enough to manifest its presence within lower-density temporal bubbles, we speak of emergence, mutation or explosion. This is the particular case of the emergence of a meme, for example a technological innovation, which at a given moment will emerge and bend space-time more strongly than the others. You can see this phenomenon almost every day. For example, a news item relayed by all the media creates a time bubble whose density, at a given moment, occupies the whole of space-time. You intuitively observe a temporal distortion in favor of this information bubble, which is heavier than the others. A television newscast, for example, will be entirely devoted to one event, ignoring all other news. Space-time is sufficiently distorted by this event to attract a considerable mass of individuals into the catchment area created for the occasion. On another level, the emergence of a new technological feature creates an attractor that focuses all attention and gradually modifies behavior. More than a fashion phenomenon, this is a spatio-temporal deformation, creating distinctions between those inside and those outside the catchment area created.

The acceleration of hyperinformational processes and their ever-accelerating multiplication are generating an inflation of time bubbles. They emerge and then disappear, immediately replaced by others. Trying to control them is an illusion, and obviously means condemning yourself to being quickly overwhelmed, frustrated and destabilized by the sheer scale of the task. The polymorphism of today's hyperinformational system creates ever-increasing opportunities for the emergence of time bubbles. They come from multiple, heterogeneous sources, copying and imitating each other in a perfect memetic mechanism; their lifespan is sometimes of the order of an instant. But each one modifies space-time in its own way, to a greater or lesser degree. Their occurrences are activated in increasingly numerous complex systems, superimposed one on top of the other, and at different speeds. As a result, there are ever-increasing temporal disparities within human societies. The value of time is unevenly distributed. On a global scale, developed societies are isolating themselves in their high-density time bubbles, posing the problem of exclusion. Living in different time bubbles means living behind new frontiers - temporal frontiers. At the level of the individual, time bubbles are in Darwinian competition; the densest occupy space and eliminate those of lower density.

These informational bubbles, multiplied in abundance, distort our perception of time to such an extent that today only the immediate and the present remain visible. Present time, bent by the sheer number and cumulative density of informational time bubbles, dilates, distorts and gradually encompasses past and future, the perspective of history and that of destiny, in an immense movement of attraction. And yet, the present has always been conceived as a hyphen that only took on meaning by virtue of what we could retain from the past, and what we could expect from the future. Today, however, the present is self-evident. Only the present is self-evident. "It is only self-evident by default. It imposes itself because the past, like the future, has detached itself from it, condemning it to temporal autarky[237]." The present has gradually become the only horizon. The past is no longer the guarantee of the future, and the present, at the very moment it is made, is seen as already historical, as already past. The present has embarked on a vast enterprise of colonizing the past, confusing history and memory. The present has also cast its nets towards the future, which has become immediately exigible. The future is lost in confusion, losing its project dimension, reduced to that of anticipation or hope. The present is at once dilated, *omnipresent* and absolute, but also inward-looking, closed in on an empty, castrated time, incapable of transmitting and promising. The absolute present is the most eminent consequence of

---

237. Laïdi (Zaki), *Le Sacre du présent*, Flammarion, 2000.

the anthropological mutations we are experiencing, leading to *Homo sapiens 2.0*. The present has become the exclusive pole of our frame of reference, determining us on an axis that no longer has any meaning. The present, with its chronophony of past and future, no longer has a temporal reference point. Man is submerged by immediate contingency, which brings him back to a chain of events that owe nothing to the past and are reluctant to bet on the future.

This radical change in the perception of temporality has essential cognitive consequences. The evolution of the human brain has reached a stage where man has become the only animal capable of subjectively apprehending his mental unity. This means that, despite the billions of neurons operating simultaneously in his brain, the multitudes of neuronal maps activated at the same time, despite this extreme diversity, man is capable of integrating all his activities into an experienced unity. The mind would thus be holistic in nature, capable of unifying separately acting parts within its neural system[238]. John Eccles believes that the self-aware mind does not simply passively read the operations taking place in its brain. Depending on attention, choice, interest or impulse, it can choose from among this infinity of cerebral activities, sometimes examining this, sometimes that, or even mixing together the results of reading from several different brain areas[239]. In this way, the mind unifies its own experiences. To achieve this unity, the brain must stabilize neural circuits over time. This is how it gradually accumulates memories, compares and evaluates them, and places them in a temporal unity. The unity of the self cannot exist in the absence of this *lasting* stabilization in an organized memory. Time, with its three temporal dimensions - past, present and future - is the essential factor in the unity of consciousness. The temporal upheavals generated by the irruption of hyperinformation into human life are introducing a

---

238. UTTAL (William R.), *The Psychobiology of Mind*, John Wiley & Sons Inc, 1978.
239. ECCLES (John C.), *Evolution of the Brain and the Creation of Consciousness*, *op. cit.*

new human condition, untethered from its natural time, cadenced in another temporal space. A new kind of man is emerging, perhaps a new version of *Homo sapiens*, whose major challenge will be to find unity or lose himself.

Interlude X

Cell phone from beyond the grave

In 1964, Philip K. Dick, one of the most brilliant science fiction writers of the 20th century, published a short story entitled *What the Dead Say*[240]. It told of individuals who, after death, could be revived for a time from their cryogenic sleep. They could then communicate with the living and, for the most powerful, intervene in world affairs. Information provided by the BBC and picked up by *Courrier international*[241] explains that communication from beyond the grave is not just a literary fantasy. Some of our fellow human beings - and it seems there are more and more of them around the world - are asking to be buried... with their cell phone. For those who choose cremation, they expressly request that their cell phone be placed in the urn among their ashes. Like the pharaohs of yesteryear, today's deceased wish to leave for the afterlife with the most modern means of communication. So that, just as when they were alive, they never break contact.

In just a few years, the cell phone has become an everyday consumer item, acquiring an indispensable character in the panoply of modern

---

240. DICK (Philip K.), "Ce que disent les morts", short story from *Minority Report*, Gallimard, 2006.
241. July 3, 2006.

man; it has even become a kind of prosthesis. Like eyeglasses and watches, it has become an integral part of the circle of objects chosen as extensions of the body. The success of the cell phone is largely due to its direct impact on notions of temporality. It blends human time (physical time, professional time, virtual time, etc.). The logic and modalities of this new relationship to time have consequences for both collective and individual life. It's a relatively new phenomenon, and it's accelerating daily, raising the question of its foundations and lines of tension: today's man seeks to master this time that seems to be slipping further and further out of his grasp.

The relationship with time expresses the confusion of both the individual and society; it is focused on possession and profitability; in both cases, we need to appropriate, master and possess it: to have time, to take time, to lack time, to waste time, to gain time... We are constantly trying to subdue and dominate time. Yet time is, by its very nature, elusive. On the contrary, time possesses and presses us. It is within us, counted, limited, inscribed in the narrow space beyond which lies our death. This relationship with time in today's society takes on its full meaning when seen in relation to the will to triumph over death; it is linked to a logic of survival and a logic of power. The latter is marked by the will to master time and space: the desire for ubiquity, the struggle against the divine like Jacob with the Angel, the seizure of opportunities, the desire for power.

By seeking to triumph over time, today's hurried, hyper-connected man is asserting his desire for existential ubiquity, his desire to live on as many registers as possible at once. This individual presents a very particular symptom: he wants to keep control. Of himself, of others, of the situation... To achieve this, he forces himself to take up the challenge of achieving everything within the time constraints given to him, and even beyond. Time becomes an object we want to possess, but which constantly eludes us. Time is the object of a compulsion to control, which seems to be the hallmark of our society.

When this possibility of control disappears, because the constraints of reality impose themselves and make it impossible for the individual, overwhelmed by time, to live up to the demands he has set himself, he still refuses to crack. Man wants to be his own sovereign, at war with time, beyond his death.

11. Global brain

Hyperinformation is the accelerating factor behind an immense transformation not only of mankind, but also of its societies and ecology. Information, long ignored because it was hidden deep within matter and life, now appears in all its power. Having unlocked the secrets of its digitization and replicative powers, mankind has unleashed a force they do not always understand, and which they vainly believe they can control. We still don't know clearly - will we ever? - what this force is, what its unity is, or what its significance is. Inspired by Lévi-Strauss's concept of *mana*, I propose to define hyperinformation[242] first and foremost as *an elementary entity that has no specific meaning, but which is opposed to the absence of meaning.* Before going any further, I invite you to clarify this idea, which may seem quite abstract to you.

Both Émile Durkheim, in his masterpiece, *Formes élémentaires de la vie religieuse*[243], and Marcel Mauss, in his *Essai sur le don*[244], sought to explain religion and magic by evoking bizarre terms borrowed from indigenous languages: *hau, mana, wanka, orenda,* etc. These words all refer to the same notion, that of an elemental energy or vital power.

---

242. *Cf. La Grande Confusion, op. cit.*
243. DURKHEIM (Émile), *Formes élémentaires de la vie religieuse (1912)*, PUF, 1998.
244. MAUSS (Marcel), "Essai sur le don", in *L'Année sociologique*, seconde série, 1923-1924.

These words all refer to the same notion, that of an elemental energy or vital power. In his *Anthropologie structurale*[245], Claude Lévi-Strauss takes up the notion of *mana*, asserting that all cultures, including the most advanced like our contemporary ones, possess concepts of this type. These do not necessarily correspond to archaic beliefs of a magical or religious nature. They are notions with neutral symbolic values, prior to any qualification. They resemble, for example, those you use when you can't find a precise word to describe something, so you say "thing[246]". You also say "thing" when a precise definition doesn't come to mind. *Machin is* a word that comes from *machine*, whose etymological source is the idea of strength and power. If we take *mana* away from its primitive origins, as Lévi-Strauss does, we'll see that the term not only corresponds to a spiritual force that animates the cosmos[247], but also to a symbolic value that has yet to be qualified. It is a particle of information that "is opposed to the absence of meaning, without itself comprising any determinate meaning[248]." This quantum of information would therefore be an unknown in a system of relations, a symbolic value that only takes on meaning in the exchange. When you exchange *something* through the right word, the meaning appears. *Mana* would thus be a "floating signifier", as Lévi-Strauss calls it. Like *mana*, hyperinformation would be the *x* in the equation, the *zero* in algebra, but also the *fundamental force* of exchange in mankind's semantic and memetic system. It's a fundamental force that only takes on meaning when put into relation. Hyperinformation manifests itself as a force that always remains

---

245. Lévi-Strauss (Claude), *Anthropologie structurale (1958)*, Plon, 1996.
246. This word comes from a medieval term meaning a "stroke of luck" in games of chance.
247. The vast majority of strategy video games and massively multiplayer online games use the term *mana* (originally Melanesian) to designate an entity's strength or energy. The term is used in the world's best-selling game, *World of Warcraft*, to mean "magical energy".
248. Lévi-Strauss (Claude), *ibid.*

188

physically identical, whatever the multiplicity and changes in the meanings it conveys. It is the movement of the hyperinformational force that creates and unifies meaning. The meaning created is a functional variable that depends on the structure assumed by the hyperinformational force - the substrate or medium - and the ecological context in which it operates. Hyperinformation is not associated with any particular semantic or memetic space. It can generate any of them. The hyperinformational force connects both the visible and its idea, the virtual and the real, the material and the immaterial. It knows no space. It has no borders or territory. It knows no time; its speed is unlimited. On the other hand, it is capable of creating specific time-spaces and "time bubbles". Hyperinformation has no preferred path; its force carries it through every possible circuit: technological, cultural, societal, cognitive, biological and so on. It navigates indifferently in Popper's three worlds. The dynamics of hyperinformation create the memetic ecology in which human beings live, giving it meaning and unifying it. It builds a global *super-organism* that brings together all individuals of the same species, linking their brains and all their memetic projections in a complex system.

The idea of the "superorganism" did not originate with hyperinformation. The concept has always been of interest in both scientific and non-scientific literature and, depending on the author, has taken on different natures corresponding to as many names. In fact, we can go back a long way to find the idea of an organization that integrates, in a global way, people and their activities. The history of the avatars of the super-organism concept is marked by three periods corresponding to three different approaches[249]: the organic approach, which consi-

---

[249]. On the history of the "global brain" concept, see the interesting study by Belgian academic Francis HEYLINGHEN: "Conception of a Global Brain: an Historical Review", in *Technical Forecasting and Social Change*, 2004.

ders society as a living organism, the encyclopedic approach, which envisages a universal knowledge network, and finally the "emergence" approach, which foresees the evolution of consciousness to a higher level of evolution.

The organic approach can certainly be traced back to Plato, who invented almost everything. In *The Republic*[250], he asserts that a well-organized society must be understood as a body. This idea, which likens society to a creature with its own limbs, brain and impulses, was to be reiterated again and again throughout history. In Rome, to appease the plebeians, the consul Agrippa declared that the hands could not rebel against the other organs, at the risk of destroying the body as a whole. Thomas Hobbes compares society to *Leviathan*, the sea monster of *Job* in the Old Testament[251]. In the 19th century, Herbert Spencer, one of the great founders of sociology, described society as an "organism" with a conscience[252]. However, this organic vision, which remained popular for several centuries, was challenged firstly by Marx, who saw it as a factor of counter-revolutionary immobilism, and then by the advocates of a free-market economy who felt uncomfortable with a society whose members were conceived as subordinate entities to a collective that transcended them. But at the very end of the 20th century, the same theme was revived in other forms: Joël de Rosnay proposed a global vision of society with his *Macroscope*[253], biophysicist Gregory Stock invented the *Metaman*, a superorganism made up of humans and machines[254], and the famous British futurologist James Lovelock formulated the *Gaia* hypothesis,

---

250. 462 c-d and 464 b.
251. Hobbes (Thomas), *Leviathan (1651)*, Gallimard, 2000.
252. Spencer (Herbert), *The Individual versus the State*, Bibliothèque de philosophie contemporaine, 1906.
253. Rosnay (Joël de), *Le Macroscope, vers une vision globale*, Seuil, 1975.
254. Stock (Gregory), *Metaman: The Merging of Humans and Machines into a Global Superorganism*, New York, Simon & Schuster, 1993.

according to which the Earth is a living organism in which humanity is just a cog[255].

The encyclopedic approach is on a completely different level: it corresponds to the idea of bringing together all human knowledge - in fact, all memes - and making them accessible to all. Diderot and d'Alembert are the best-known protagonists of this ambition, with their *Encyclopédie*, a brilliant symbol of the Enlightenment. But of course, as generations passed and scientific, technical and cultural advances were made, bringing together all human knowledge soon proved to be an insurmountable task. In the first decades of the 20th century, however, one man confronted this difficulty. Although he did not enjoy the notoriety that would have enabled his name to stand the test of time, he nevertheless invented the science of bibliography, which was to become the science of information. He is the Belgian Paul Otlet, considered perhaps the visionary inventor of the Internet, and certainly of *Wikipedia*, the Web's gigantic encyclopedia. Indeed, his ambition was to realize "a universal and perpetual Encyclopedia", with as collaborators "all the scholars of all times and all countries." In his *Traité de documentation*[256], published in 1934, he envisaged a scenario for the future of books and documentation that leaves us, contemporaries of the early 21st century, accustomed to surfing the Internet, perfectly dreamy. He imagines the following scene: "The work table would no longer be laden with books. In their place stands a screen and within reach a telephone. Over there, in the distance, in an immense building, are all the books and all the information... From there, the page to be read would appear on the screen to find out the answer to the questions asked by telephone, with or without wires. A screen would be doubled, quadrupled or decupled if the aim

---

255. LOVELOCK (James E.), *The Earth is a Living Being. The Gaia Hypothesis*, Éditions du Rocher, 1990.
256. OTLET (Paul), *Traité de documentation*, Éditions du Centre de lecture publique de la Communauté française de Belgique, 1989.

was to multiply the number of texts and documents to be compared simultaneously; there would be a loudspeaker if sight was to be aided by hearing. Utopia today, because it doesn't yet exist anywhere, but it could well become reality if our methods and instrumentation are further perfected. And this improvement could go as far as making it automatic to call up documents on the screen...". Don't forget that this text was written in 1934, at a time when computers didn't exist, let alone the transmission of digital data over a network. Around the same time, the famous science-fiction writer Herbert George Wells envisioned the *world brain*, which would correspond to the idea of a permanent encyclopedia of the world. He envisaged a global synthesis of bibliography and documentation, indexed and updated all the time - not yet in "real time". This would be a "complete planetary memory, accessible to everyone[257]". A little later, in 1945, the American engineer Vannevar Bush, who left his name in history for his participation in the development of the atomic bomb, invented something more peaceful: the notion of hypermedia. Under the name *Memex,* he christened a system enabling users to store documents of all kinds - books, pictures, personal notes, etc. - and to associate them freely according to need. As computers were still in their infancy at the time, it wasn't until the 1960s that Theodore Nelson and Douglas Englebart pioneered hypertext. But it was in 1991 that the old dream finally came true, with Tim Berners-Lee founding the *World Wide Web* by combining a simplified format for hypertext documents, HTML, well known today, and a universal scheme for locating documents, the "URL[258]" address. The Internet was born with a vocation: to distribute information around the world, freely and easily, via an interactive

---

257. WELLS (Herbert G.), *World Brain*, London, Ayer Co Publications, 1938.
258. BERNERS-LEE (Tim), *Weaving the Web: The Original Design and Ultimate Destiny of the World Wide Web by Its Inventor*, Harper Business, 2000.

192

network of personal computers. Philosopher Pierre Lévy liked to call this super-organism *cyberspace*[259].

The third approach to superorganism is that of *emergence*. It concentrates both spiritual and speculative dimensions, and crystallizes in the eminent figure of evolutionary paleontologist and Jesuit Father Pierre Teilhard de Chardin. The author of *Phénomène humain* was probably one of the first[260] to develop a cosmology that distinguishes between the three elements of the geosphere, the biosphere and the *noosphere*, which he sees as a thin film surrounding the Earth, containing all of humanity's knowledge and capacity for thought - "an immense thinking machine". Teilhard is a proponent of the theory of evolution; but in his view, contrary to widespread opinion, evolution did not end with the appearance of the human zoological type. It continues, even today, according to the law of increasing complexity. Not only has evolution not come to a standstill, but it is moving on to a new phase, that of the general rise of consciousness. He writes: "The network and consciousness of a *Noosphere is* being woven around us - beyond any unity recognized or even foreseen by biology up to now", adding in a note: "The Noosphere combines in itself the properties of a planetary sheet ("sphere") and those of a kind of superior individuality, endowed with a kind of superconsciousness[261]". In January 1947, Teilhard de Chardin, an extraordinary anticipator of our contemporary "hyperworld", asserted: "Unquestionably, at an ever-accelerating

---

259. Lévy (Pierre), *L'Intelligence collective, op. cit.*

260. In fact, Teilhard de Chardin was inspired by the Russian geologist Vladimir Vernadsky (1863-1945), who had proposed a model for our planet made up of different interacting layers: the lithosphere, the atmosphere, the biosphere, the technosphere and the *noosphere*, or sphere of thought. The Jesuit father also worked closely with the philosopher Édouard Le Roy, who can legitimately be considered the co-author of the noosphere concept. [Cf. Le Roy (Édouard), *Les Origines humaines et l'évolution de l'intelligence*, Boivin et Cie, 1931].

261. Teilhard de Chardin (Pierre), "Le rebondissement humain de l'évolution" (1948), in *L'Avenir de l'homme*, Seuil, 1959.

speed, the network (a worldwide network) of economic and psychic ties is weaving itself around us, enclosing us and penetrating us ever more closely. Every day, it becomes more and more impossible for us to act or think in any way other than in solidarity[262]." The irresistible force of this movement has a meaning, which Teilhard reveals as follows: "What does this great event mean? For my part, I can see only one explanation. It is that the enormous excess of free energy released by the redeployment of the Noosphere is naturally, evolutionarily, destined to flow into the construction and functioning of what I have called its 'brain'... Humanity is progressively becoming 'cephalized'... Before our very eyes, humanity is weaving its brain[263]."

Teilhard de Chardin's ideas have fertilized many others. With the acceleration of the hyperinformational force, the metaphor of the global brain takes on a new tone, as it builds, before our very eyes, a superorganism of an unprecedented nature, at an unprecedented speed. In the same way that memetics brings to light replicants with a quasi-biological grain, whereas previously we only saw exchanges of words and images, the concept of the superorganism leads us to take another look at the relationships that are established in human social systems, as well as at the evolution of man as a species. There are fundamental generative mechanisms that go beyond the history of mankind, since they are part of processes that link them to the history of the universe in general and of life in particular. That's why I spoke to you at the beginning of this book about the tendency of elementary organisms to group together, to establish cooperative relationships and eventually *symbioses*, thus setting in motion informational living chains, increasingly extended in size, but also in complexity. This is how multi-cellular organisms appeared in the

---

262. Teilhard de Chardin (Pierre), "La formation de la 'Noosphère'" (1947), in *L'Avenir de l'homme*, Seuil, 1959.
263. *Ibid.*

primordial broth of life, and this is how memes organize themselves, aggregating and complementing each other to form sets of ideas, cultures, civilizations and worlds. Symbiosis is certainly the source of a powerful evolutionary current leading from the simplest forms of life to the most accomplished superorganisms, and to the most complex brains, whether human, artificial or hybrid. As soon as life appeared on Earth, 4.5 billion years ago, a process was set in motion, interconnecting the multiple networks of living organisms into a single system - the biosphere. Human beings, their societies and human projections are part of this long river of evolution. Our electronic networks, the Internet, cell phones, geolocation and all our most advanced information technologies are but avatars among others in this evolutionary process. For "the survival of consciousness and intelligence does not depend on the particular nature of the material that supports them, but on the complexity of the arrangement of this material[264]." Like living organisms, the technologies invented by man undergo Darwinian selection, with the most suitable having the best chance of developing. Like living organisms, they unfold within the framework of complex adaptive systems, in which convergences, amplifications, hybridizations and mutations are the main drivers of progress. Like living organisms, they unfold in networks, webs and systems of connected intelligences, gradually forming, through self-organization and self-learning, increasingly evolved systems, super-organisms, even a global brain. Memes are the active agents of this evolution; it is they, driven by hyperinformational flows, that are building, brick by brick, brain by brain, these increasingly intimately connected superorganisms. "Here grows something greater than we are[265]" observed Nietzsche. Indeed, our contemporaries are witnessing the rapid emergence of the equivalent of a vast distributed

---

264. THUAN (Trinh Xuan), *La Mélodie secrète*, Gallimard, 1991.
265. NIETZSCHE (Friedrich), *Aurore (1881)*, Gallimard, 1989.

brain, carrying humanity's knowledge, ideas and cultures, as well as its passions, whims and interconnected madness, potentially available to everyone, at any time, everywhere.

What do a bacterial colony, a swarm of bees, a flock of starlings, a pack of wolves, a school of sardines or a human society have in common? They are superorganisms, i.e. living systems of a higher order whose components are themselves organisms. They are coherent and cannot be reduced to groups of isolated individuals. Biologists agree that many insect colonies are superorganisms. They behave like multicellular biological organisms, with each cell dependent on the other. Human organisms, on the other hand, are more specific, for two reasons. The first is that each human being - considered as an individual cell - can live separately from the group. Unlike insect societies, human societies are in fact ambivalent, allowing conflicts between collective stakes and individual egoisms to persist more or less explicitly. Human societies therefore "pretend" that the superorganism has an identity[266], which inevitably leads to providing it with one. The second reason is that the human superorganism combines, in a symbiotic process, humans and their memetic projections, notably artificial machines. The human species is thus in the process of producing a superorganism whose level of organization is superior to its own entity. The challenge is unprecedented. Joël de Rosnay predicts: "No political, philosophical or even religious approach has prepared us for this titanic task, which calls into question man's sovereignty and the scope of his action on the world[267]."

Since Maturana and Varela, we know that life is an *autopoietic* system, i.e. a system in which recursive relations, organized in networks,

---

266. Some authors refer to this characteristic of human societies as "collective *stance*". Cf. Gaines (Brian R.), "The Collective Stance in Modeling Expertise in Individuals and Organizations", in *International Journal of Expert Systems*, n° 71, pp. 22-51, 1994.
267. Rosnay (Joël de), *L'Homme symbiotique, op. cit.*

196

produce their own elements, and sustain the whole in relation to its environment[268]. A superorganism is typically an autopoietic system, capable of autonomy, responsible for its own "maintenance" and growth. More fundamentally, the global brain can be understood as a living entity that has reached a higher level of evolution. The evolution I'm talking about here has its origins in the depths of the ages, its sources at the heart of elementary particles. This evolution does not follow a linear path, nor is its speed one-dimensional. It takes place in a multidimensional space-time, shaped by the emergence of time bubbles of different densities. The global brain being built today from within our living system, without any overall plan, without any real intention, in a chaotic way, is developing at an accelerated speed. Its time scale is no longer that of centuries or millennia, but that of a man's life - a few years, or even a handful of hours. The emergence of a system of such complexity generates skills that exceed those of each of its components[269]. Hyperinformation accelerates this phenomenon. It is giving rise to a global intelligence that is still rudimentary today, but which gives a glimpse of the proportions and forms it will take tomorrow.

The Internet is undoubtedly a rough prefiguration of the global brain that is taking shape before our very eyes. The Web can simply be defined as a hypermedia interface capable of processing information. It can integrate a considerable number of documents and information, distributing them instantaneously across the entire planet, without regard to borders or space. It is fed by information produced by individuals who don't know each other, and who may never have had the slightest relationship. In such a network, the main

268. *Cf.* MATURANA (Humberto) & VARELA (Francisco), *Autopoiesis and Cognition: The Realization of the Living, op. cit.*
269. *Valentin Turchin speaks of* metasystem transition, *cf.* The Phenomenon of Science, a Cybernetic Approach to Human Evolution, *New York, Colombia University Press, 1977.*

characteristic of information is not its location, but its associative power. It's the hypertext links that connect the information to each other, in the same way as synapses connect neurons in the brain. Each link has the potential to excite a new "neural map", in other words, a new information space. In this way, the Web functions as a gigantic memory available to human beings. However, the brain is not simply a memory; it dynamically arranges information in its memories. This function is the very process of learning and thinking. When a human brain *learns*, it organizes the information it receives in the form of neuronal associations, through successive learning or imitation. Those that are most frequently used are retained, while others are eliminated, forgotten or erased from consciousness. I explained that in the early stages of a child's learning, the number of neurons in the brain diminishes as a result of this selective sorting. When the human brain *thinks*, it associates neuronal maps through a process of conceptual integration. The concepts that emerge are more or less rich, depending on the strength of the associations that form them. This mechanism enables the brain to demonstrate its creativity, its ability to associate different concepts and discover new ones it has never encountered before. The Web has the potential to work in the same way. In this respect, artificial intelligence specialists are very interested in a law discovered in 1949 by a Canadian neuropsychologist, Donald Hebb. Hebb's law states that two neurons activated together strengthen their connection in such a way as to facilitate future activation. This characteristic is the very foundation of all learning and knowledge acquisition[270]. This rule also states that if a group of neurons is repeatedly and jointly stimulated, this group will form an "assembly of cells" that will remain activated for a longer

---

270. Hebb (Donald O.), *The Organization of Behavior: A Neuropsychological Theory*, New York, Wiley, 1949.

or shorter time after the stimulus[271]. Remarkably, Hebb's law applies perfectly to the Internet. When you surf websites today, you follow links that have been fabricated by the site designers. They are the result of human manipulation. If you follow the same link several times in a row, it may be assumed that this link has more weight than the others. Links you never click on may be considered useless. Researchers have developed a system that automatically creates new hyperlinks whenever it considers that they are likely to offer a route that web users will take. It will gradually close links that are no longer relevant because they are not sufficiently solicited. The *Google* search engine works in a similar way, offering search results sorted according to popularity and the number of links pointing to a site. These techniques are inspired by Hebb's law, and pave the way for a fully collaborative Web that learns to respond to us in a "hypertinent[272]" way. The information available on the Web is thus structured in a gigantic associative network that continually "learns" according to the behavior of its users. It can then "think" and act intelligently by proposing information that the user was not aware of, but which is likely to be of interest to him or her, depending on his or her characteristics. This is the case, for example, with *Amazon, the* online bookseller that is able to offer its customers books that match their interests because it has implemented a learning process that "learns" its users' tastes from their behavior on the site. It can thus "advise", "suggest" relatively relevant recommendations to its users. I use these terms in quotation marks, because it's obvious that *Amazon*'s primary motivation is to sell. The fact remains, however, that the technologies

---

271. Twenty years after this discovery, researchers developed the idea with the theory of "long-term synaptic potentiation", which plays a fundamental role in memory function and demonstrates the extreme plasticity of brain organization.
272. HEYLINGHEN (Francis) & BOLLEN (Johan), "The World Wide Web as a Super Brain: from metaphor to model", in *Cybernetics and Systems*, Austrian Society for Cybernetics, 1996 (pespmc1.vub.ac.be/Papers/WWWSuperBRAIN.html).

implemented are a prelude to the implementation of an increasingly intelligent information network. What we need to understand is that the system feeds itself from the actions of its members. Typically, we're dealing with an organization configured as a living, cooperative network. The value of the Internet, the relevance of its content and organization, comes not from any institution, but from the cooperative action of hundreds of millions of contributors, hundreds of millions of human brains, real neurons permanently connected to the global brain.

Peer-to-peer technologies, which can be called "peer-to-peer", "peer-to-peer" or "P2P", are a further step towards the global brain. Under this system, the computer connected to the Internet is not only a client, but also a server. To use the analogy of the human brain, *peer-to-peer has the* same effect as if you were able to transfer the entire contents of your brain to that of a friend. I won't drag this metaphor out any longer - you're going to have nightmares. We wondered in a previous chapter how memes could jump from one brain to another, but with *peer-to-peer,* they've found a royal road. *Peer-to-peer was* originally conceived as a distributed computing system, not an information-sharing technology. The idea was based on the observation that a considerable amount of computing power was not being used by individual computers. Yet this power could be reclaimed to carry out calculations that require very large numbers of operations. In 1999, researchers at the University of California, Berkeley, came up with the idea of pooling this immense unused computing power, which you leave fallow when you're not using your computer, to... search for extraterrestrials. The SETI (*Search Extra Terrestrial Intelligence*) project involves using the processors of millions of computers connected to the Internet to analyze and decrypt the signals that a non-terrestrial intelligence might emit, voluntarily or otherwise, from its planet of origin. The project was so successful that many other programs were launched in a wide variety of fields: climatology, medical research, mathematics, economics - wherever important calculations had to be made[273]. The idea of pooling personal computers for scientific purposes soon evolved into a technology that enabled not only computing time to be shared, but also computer content and files to be pooled. The first application dates back to June 1999, with the famous *Napster* website. Its inventor, 18-year-old student Shawn Fanning, simply wanted to share his favorite music tracks with his friends. He devised a program for downloading music files, leaving the files stored on his computer freely available. The craze was such that within two years, *Napster* was being used by over 23 million people worldwide. This free sharing of music between millions of fans did not go unnoticed by the major record companies, who took legal action to shut down the network. But *Napster was* to have a following, and today there are dozens of ways of sharing music, videos, information and files of all kinds, using *peer-to-peer* technologies. The most important thing to remember is that this technology was originally designed for fun. Its success and appropriation are due to the millions of users who spontaneously connected to each other, forming vast neural communities. *Peer-to-peer* demonstrates the power of the network that innervates the global brain, when collective passion and the pleasure of cooperation take hold. The first *peer-to-peer* applications transformed the Internet into cooperative networks sharing computing power and files. But new generations of network technologies are emerging, and their uses are taking us a step closer to the global brain, by sharing thoughts, decisions and opinions. Blogs, wikis and RSS feeds are just some of the applications moving in this direction. Constantly, at any time of the day or night, across continents, languages and cultures, hundreds of millions of individual brains upload information to the global system from their PCs, cell phones, webcams, PDAs... Every

---

273. Projects are updated and available for consultation on the *Berkeley Open Infrastructure for Network Computing* website (http://boinc.berkeley.edu/).

document, photo, film, e-mail, text, note or comment uploaded to the global brain creates new ideas, new memes stored in its memories. Every act of an Internet user modifies and reprograms the superorganism from within. Every link followed, every favorite saved, every e-mail address added strengthens its synaptic links. Every modified site, completed blog, expanded wiki, updated podcast, enriches the content available to all.

What emerges is the project of a varied intelligence, distributed everywhere, constantly enhanced and pooled at all times. A "collective intelligence", perhaps. But which of the global brain, the group or the individuals that make it up, has become more informed, more reactive, more intelligent? Is there such a thing as collective consciousness? Is the global brain merely the more or less heterogeneous sum of individual consciousnesses? Are our individual brains doomed to merge into this immense community magma? Is the collective intelligence that emerges truly an "augmented" intelligence, and for whose benefit?

Interlude XI

The Wikipedia case

"I'm a *Wikipedia* enthusiast[274]. *Wikipedia is* criticized for not producing information, but neither do teachers. *Wikipedia* is a transmitter of knowledge. A transmitter. Like teachers, like journalists... Of course there are errors, but no more than in the Encyclopaedia *Britannica.* The number of errors contained in the books of the Bibliothèque nationale de France is gigantic. Who checks the content of these books? Who corrects the errors? On *Wikipedia,* the truth is re-established by anonymous, free volunteers. In newspapers, errors are recycled from article to article. Out of a hundred articles written about my books, ninety-nine of them gave the impression that the author hadn't read my work. People ask me if I check *Wikipedia.* Do I check all the dictionaries I consult? No. I only check the Académie dictionary, because that's my job.

Even if there are mistakes, *Wikipedia* works. Today, there's a free encyclopedia accessible to everyone. What does it matter that this encyclopedia was created by people from the IT world? Printing was invented by people who knew about lead, writing by people who discovered marble...

---

274. Text by Michel Serres, Académie française, published in *Le Point,* June 21, 2007.

I use *Wikipedia*. Everyone uses it. Why distrust it? Today, any invention triggers negative questions. People ask: is it dangerous? Is it serious? *Wikipedia* is libertarian, collective and free. What could be more generous? *Wikipedia* gives us confidence in what a human group can be.

This is a company that is not run by experts. The time when people who know explain from the top of their knowledge to those who don't know is over. The time for science democracy has arrived. Today, oncology professors are learning from cancer patients' blogs. This is the time of reverse education. With *Wikipedia*, knowledge is not transmitted from the top down, but shared. The teacher in a lecture, the priest from the pulpit, PPDA on the TV set - it's all the same, and it's all over. Knowledge is not power. It's a treasure to be shared. This is what the Web makes possible, and *Wikipedia* is one of the components of this evolution. We have to stop waiting for knowledge to fall from on high. Knowledge spouted by experts gives me a rash. You have to learn unconditionally, uncritically. I'm sick to death of critical thinking. The only real intellectual act is invention. Criticism is easy, invention is difficult. Criticism is an act of resentment. Invention moves forward. And so much the worse for all our prophets of doom."

12. Enhanced intelligence

Examples of animal intelligence have always fascinated mankind, who have long been convinced that they have exclusive rights in this field. Among animal species, one that has been studied more than any other is the ant. It's true that they are sufficiently common and distributed across all latitudes to facilitate observations. Another reason may be that ants are our direct demographic competitors on our planet. Their total biomass is equal to that of all human beings combined, which, given their size, represents billions of individuals. Some science-fiction writers have gone so far as to say that ants will be our successors should man one day disappear from the Earth[275]. What's fascinating about ants - but the same phenomenon can be found in many other animal species - is their collective intelligence. Indeed, they are capable of making collective life eminently profitable for the species; this is even the key to their survival and deployment. I won't go into a lengthy account of the life of ants, which would go far beyond the scope of this book. This subject has been studied at

---

275. Well-known scientist Claude Allègre believes that only insects will be able to replace man when he disappears from the face of the Earth. He's not thinking of ants, but rather of a flying social insect, a hybrid mutant of wasp and bee. Cf. ALLÈGRE (Claude), *Introduction à une Histoire naturelle*, Fayard, 1992.

length by eminent scientists[276]. What we need to remember is the mastery these insects have developed in implementing a sophisticated information network, giving rise to a particularly complex social system. The lives of ants are of interest to specialists in intelligence, whether human or artificial, because these little creatures have developed highly flexible and durable problem-solving solutions. Yet their day-to-day problems are many and varied. The life of an ant is no picnic: foraging, nest building, division of labor, distribution of tasks between individuals, and so on. To solve all these challenges, an individual's intelligence is totally inadequate, because his or her cognitive development is very limited. Only collective intelligence, i.e. intelligence capable of functioning without external control or central coordination mechanism, enables them to achieve feats that an isolated individual could not face alone. These insects have no awareness of the global superorganism they are building. They do so without the help of any conductor or prior plan. This is possible because their functioning is based on a decentralized logic, centered on the cooperation of autonomous units. You've no doubt observed queues of ants seemingly heading towards a specific goal, presumably a food source. Well, the path chosen by the ant colony is not programmed in advance. It's the result of a large number of direct or indirect interactions between individuals, who have the ability to deposit chemical substances - pheromones - along their route, acting as messages for the other members of the colony. Each individual deposits the same message on the trail. In this way, information is passed from individual to individual, without each ant needing to be aware of the entire path[277]. They pass on, as it were, a witness, without

---

276. See in particular: Passera (Luc), *La Véritable Histoire des fourmis*, Fayard, 2006 and Keller (Laurent) & Gordon (Élisabeth), *La Vie des fourmis*, Odile Jacob, 2006.
277. Cf. Bonabeau (Éric) & Theraulaz (Guy), "Swarm Smarts", in *Scientific American*, n° 282, p. 72-79, 2000.

knowing where it will lead them[278]. But all of these interactions lead to the emergence of new properties at colony level. It's not the ants that are intelligent, but the super-organism they form that is. The collective intelligence of ants is an interesting model for understanding what a collective human intelligence might become in the age of hyperinformation. Indeed, the exponential increase in informational exchanges between humans is creating the conditions for the emergence of an increasingly complex world. We'll come back to this later. In such a complex world, the selection of relevant and useful information takes on vital strategic importance for decision-making. All things considered, man finds himself in a situation analogous to that of an ant: he often has only a very partial perception of the data involved in a problem, and must advance step by step in the discovery process, choosing between numerous and sometimes contradictory avenues. Individual intelligence is not enough to fully integrate the overall project. When you're doing research on the Internet, you're bound to feel like you're groping your way through the hyperlinks that present themselves to you, without knowing *a priori* what you're going to find. The example of the information processing system that ants have taken a hundred million years to perfect could well be a way of thinking about the emergence of more reliable, flexible and robust human or artificial intelligence systems[279].

Collective intelligence has existed for as long as man has lived in society. You no doubt experience it regularly, whether in your work meetings, your club or sports activities, or in the think tanks you may participate in. These experiences of collective intelligence generally take place in small assemblies of individuals, and in a restricted spatial environment. In these day-to-day situations, you may have seen a

---

278. This is what specialists call *stigmergy*, a class of mechanisms that enable insects to coordinate their activities through indirect interactions.
279. Cf. THERAULAZ (Guy), "L'intelligence collective", in *L'Intelligence*, Jacques Lautrey and Jean-François Richard (dir.), Lavoisier, 2005.

number of phenomena emerge. In a soccer team, for example, you've observed that each player has his or her own talents, but in the course of a match, the team acts as a homogeneous entity, coordinating itself without the information between players following an explicit hierarchical path. A soccer team functions as a complex system that self-regulates according to its environment, in this case, the actions of the opposing team. Whether it's a soccer team, a choir or a work meeting, in all cases a process of "natural" collective intelligence occurs, with a number of recurring characteristics. Four of them stand out. The first is the emergence of a "higher unit". Every choir, every soccer team has its own particular style and character. In some cases, we even speak of a "spirit", associating personal qualities with a group made up of several individuals. You'll then notice the emergence of a new space, which Jean-François Noubel calls "holoptic space[280]". This is a three-dimensional space that allows you to perceive the manifestations of other members of the group, as well as visualizing the overall emerging figure. Holoptism is a multi-dimensional figure that corresponds well to the dynamics of collective intelligence. Its opposite is *panopticism*, in which all information converges towards a central point of control. A third characteristic is implicit or explicit agreement between group members. Everyone must accept a minimum set of rules for the group to function harmoniously. Finally, you'll note a fourth characteristic: the existence of a "project", i.e. an objective shared by all. This could be, for example, the desire to achieve a concrete result at the end of a work meeting, or to win the match for a soccer team. These characteristics apply to situations where the groups are small and operate in an identified environment. When groups are very large and evolve in networks whose architecture transcends them, the four principles become problematic. In the context of the

---

280. Noubel (Jean-François), *Intelligence collective, la révolution invisible*, TheTransitioner.org, 2006.

super-organisms that are emerging as a result of hyperinformation, the founding principles of natural collective intelligence need to be profoundly amended and clarified.

The first principle concerns the emergence of a collective personality, a "spirit", a "collective conscience", we might say. It's true that, in certain circumstances, human groupings give rise to new characteristics of a collective nature, which didn't exist at the level of each individual. A crowd, for example, is typically a concrete social whole, possessing a "psychology" that can be finely analyzed. This was done by psychologists, among whom Gustave Le Bon was a precursor. In the very first chapter of his famous *Psychology of Crowds*, he writes: "A collective soul is formed, transient no doubt, but with very clear characteristics. The collectivity then becomes what, for want of a better expression, I'll call an organized crowd, or, if one prefers, a psychological crowd. It forms a single being, and is subject to the law of the mental unity of crowds." In a crowd, whatever the individuals that make it up, whether they are alike or not, intelligent or not, whatever their way of life, "the mere fact that they are transformed into a crowd, endows them with a kind of collective soul." Thus, in such a gathering of human beings, the phenomenon is not one of aggregation alone, but of combination: a new being is born, endowed with properties different from those of the bodies that served to constitute it. A crowd perfectly fits the definition of a superorganism. However, the conclusion reached by these analyses in no way reveals the "intelligence" of crowds. Quite the opposite, in fact. Le Bon writes, without in any way qualifying his remarks: "Crowds accumulate not intelligence, but mediocrity." Indeed, in a crowd, the individual feels irresponsible, giving in to instincts that he or she alone would have tended to curb. On the other hand, crowds are subject to "mental contagion" - René Girard would call it "mimicry" - which leads individuals to forget their common sense and sometimes sacrifice their personal interests for those of the group. Finally, in a crowd, the individual is hypnotized, subject to a form of suggestibility that can lead him to undertake actions he would not have been able to carry out alone. As Gustave Le Bon put it: "By the very fact that he is part of a crowd, man descends several degrees on the scale of civilization[281]". Numerous psychologists have developed this work. Their experiments, conducted in crowds as well as in work groups and think tanks, mostly reveal the pitfalls of collective thinking; in some cases, they even speak of a "loss of spirit[282]".

Is the expression "collective intelligence" just an antilogy? In a collective, would intelligence go down a notch? Yet there are many situations where the contribution of different knowledge and points of view produces a renewed and more "intelligent" vision of a problem. The breaking point between enhanced and diminished intelligence certainly lies in the ability of the group, understood in the broadest sense of the term, i.e. the superorganism, to endow itself with a "collective consciousness" of a higher order. We have observed that the higher consciousness of human beings only emerged with the mastery of social exchanges through language, and developed in particular through memetic enrichment. The question now is whether a super-organism made up of individuals intensely interconnected by hyperinformational flows can gradually acquire sufficient knowledge to acquire a collective consciousness and bring about the emergence of real collective intelligence. The global brain we described in the previous chapter is of a completely different nature to the individual brains that make it up. It connects individual brains via memetic

---

281. Le Bon (Gustave), *Psychologie des foules*, PUF, 1947.
282. See, for example, Salomon Asch's experiments on the role of social influence (*Groups, Leadership and Men*, Pittsburgh, Carnegie Press, 1951) or Irving Janis's on the perverse effects of *groupthinking* in the US government (*Groupthink. Psychological Studies of Policies Decisions and Fiascoes*, Boston, Houghton Mifflin Company, 1982). Christian Morel's analysis of air disasters reveals the same phenomena of aberration (*Les Décisions absurdes. Sociologie des erreurs radicales et persistantes*, Gallimard, 2002).

information channels, forming a vast network whose performance is considerably enhanced, both in terms of power and diversity. The exchanges circulating in this network store innumerable models of knowledge, which are relatively easily accessible and available to successive generations. Gerald Edelman has explained how, thanks to Darwinian selection, neuronal structures emerge and organize themselves in the human brain[283]. In the same way, the global brain is structured by the contributions of the individuals connected to it, constituting vast bases of available knowledge, in constant construction and deconstruction. In this process, which of the superorganism or the individuals that make it up has become more informed, more responsive, more intelligent, and ultimately, conscious? Probably both. In any case, the superorganism has acquired something more, and the individuals that make it up have the ability to benefit from it. However, if we take a broader look, we can give a clearer answer to this question. The exponential growth of hyperinformation creates a self-enriching, self-complexifying brain. The superorganism emerges without any external higher consciousness having decided to do so. It is self-generating, but it must remain open, i.e. it must allow individual consciousnesses to find in it the source of new enrichment. In the pages that follow, we shall gradually see that this is not so obvious.

The second characteristic of natural collective intelligence is *holoptism*, i.e. the ability to be spatially aware of the actions of the other individuals making up the group, but also of the group itself in its unity. In the hyperinformational global brain, is holoptism still possible? Are we, the human neurons of a global brain, capable of representing ourselves as actors, and can we become aware not only of the super-organism we form, but also of the space in which we evolve? This requires a prodigious effort, because since Protagoras

---

283. I'm referring here to the "Theory of Neuron Group Selection".

2,500 years ago, we've been used to "man being the measure of all things". However, with the emergence of the hyper-informational global brain, our image of man is no longer on the normal scale, the one we learned from classical psychology, but also from the simplest experiences acquired at school or at home. It's virtually impossible for us to internalize the consequences of the emergence of such a superorganism, which extends our intellectual and sensory capacities far beyond our body's natural capabilities. *Homos sapiens* has changed scale on every level: temporal, but also spatial. The space in which we live has changed radically since the development of hyperinformation. The change is not that of globalization or economic globalization, which is merely an epiphenomenon, or at least the appearance of a more radical mutation. Our space has lost its distance. Its rough edges have been stripped away to create a surface that is supple and elastic in places, rigid and petrified in others. Several *organic* spaces are superimposed one on top of the other, folds and flat surfaces intertwined. They are generated and generated again, perpetually, by human activity. They are all in action, with each other and in relation to each other. Evolving daily in a teeming eruption of complex spaces, *Homo sapiens* of the 21st century is losing his usual landmarks, his familiar horizons, his eternally known territory. Every day, our living space is pierced by flows that cut and recompose it. Human and informational fluids, those of material and immaterial goods, ideas, fashions and merchandise, deny distance and create new, fluid and shifting architectures. The space that emerges is that of the *network*, in which place becomes an interconnection. The geometry of network actors becomes multidimensional: it integrates, with great mobility, position in the network and connections to the network. In this configuration, holoptism is an almost impossible task for a normally constituted individual. His space is fragmented into several spaces that are not necessarily separate, but which meet and interact with each other in very different ways: inclusion, exclusion, insertion, integration, differentiation, enclosure. *Homo sapiens,* connected by hyperinformation to the global brain, is challenged to invent new coherences in multiple spaces. He must seek balance in a fluid logic, in spaces whose levels are multiplied, spaces that are mobile, dynamic, interconnected, extremely sensitive and reactive.

The third characteristic of natural collective intelligence concerns the existence of a kind of "contract" binding the members of the group. How is this possible in the superorganism we're discovering? First of all, let's remember that a superorganism is a *complex* system that obeys its own logic. It can't be expected to be loyal to its members - a complex system isn't set up that way. German sociologist Niklas Luhmann explains that such a functional system is by nature closed in on itself and its own efficiency[284]. It is therefore perfectly impossible for it to take into account what does not depend on it, and to observe the effects of its actions on individuals and on the group as a whole. If it were to do so, it would limit itself and risk compromising its own existence. Such a system is *self-referential,* i.e. it refers exclusively to itself and considers its environment from its own point of view. This selective blindness can only cease when the superorganism is able to broaden its perspective by becoming aware of its identity not only in relation to itself, but also in relation to its constituent entities and its future identity. Assuming that a superorganism is capable of this virtue, it's easy to see how its members would coordinate and relate to each other naturally, according to almost natural rules. In a way, the superorganism would govern itself. This can only happen if the superorganism has reached a higher level of *intelligence.* You may say that we're not there yet. And you'd be wrong. In fact, even today, when the global brain is still at an embryonic stage, we can observe spontaneous systems of regulation and contractualization between the humans that

---

284. Cf. LUHMANN (Niklas), *Politique et complexité,* Cerf, 1999.

make it up. Coordination models based on quasi-contractual logics of cooperation and reputation are emerging.

Cooperation presupposes the implementation of mechanisms for reducing complexity that are reciprocal, i.e. accepted by all parties. The aim of these mechanisms is, on the one hand, to bring about relative self-limitation and consideration of others, and, on the other, to establish a medium- or long-term perspective. The cornerstone of these complexity-reduction mechanisms is the seemingly trivial notion of *trust*. In a complex super-organism made up of highly differentiated individuals, trust is the key driver of coordination. Indeed, it has a characteristic that makes it particularly operative: it absorbs uncertainty by making it tolerable. Niklas Luhmann describes the link between trust and cooperation very clearly: "The world is spread out in uncontrollable complexity, so that other humans can freely choose between very different actions at any time. But I must act here and now. [...] I would have a better chance of achieving a more complex rationality if I could place my trust in a certain future behavior of others (or contemporary or past, but for me determinable only in the future). If I can trust that I will benefit from the success of the action, then I can afford forms of cooperation that do not pay off immediately and are not immediately available to me. If I rely on the fact that others will act in concert with me, or refrain from doing so, I can follow my own self-interest more rationally[285]." In a logic of cooperation, the action of differentiated, "selfish[286]" and self-referential entities changes radically. Each entity now sees its own interests in the interests of the other and of the whole. As a result, the relationships that emerge are more partnership-based, with everyone agreeing to make their contribution to the super-organism in order to

---

285. LUHMANN (Niklas), *Trust, a mechanism for reducing social complexity*, Economica, 2006.
286. AXELROD (Robert), *Comment réussir dans un monde d'égoïstes*, Odile Jacob, 1996.

improve the way cooperation works. The logic of this type of action is to decentralize and network knowledge, with the aim of increasing the positive effects for each party and for the system as a whole. In this framework of collective intelligence, trust plays its full role as a complexity reducer, enabling each party to accept risks in return for the prospect of future benefits. It's a give-and-take strategy, where everyone knows that one day, they could be a winner.

This is exactly the strategy that is already emerging in the rudimentary global brain that is the Internet. I've already mentioned *peer-to-peer* technology, which is nothing other than a cooperative process that you may have observed to have generated itself as if spontaneously. What makes the emergence of cooperation possible is the existence, in the eyes of the superorganism's participants, of a "pooled resource". This is the super-organism's social capital, seen as something that belongs to everyone. It is therefore in everyone's interest to make it bear fruit, and to self-regulate and sanction deviant practices. In this context, trust - the cornerstone of cooperation - is underpinned by the concept of "reputation". Let's take a concrete example: *eBay*. It's one of the most visited websites in the world. Its business is the auction of goods of all kinds offered by private individuals. In simple terms, it's a huge flea market, a virtual marketplace where consumers buy and sell from each other. *eBay* currently has over 200 million registered members and offers tens of millions of different items for sale. For the system to work, i.e. for Internet users to agree to buy an item from someone they don't know, *eBay* has set up a reputation system for both sellers and buyers. Everyone is rated according to their trading history. Buyers can thus see the seriousness and reliability of the seller, but sellers can also judge the seriousness of their buyers. The system, which generates several billion dollars in sales, operates on a very large scale, based on a self-generated trust mechanism that is exceptionally robust. Other examples of this type, certainly on a different scale, exist on the Web. They are all based on the exchange of *opinions* shared in real time by millions of people worldwide. This completely transforms the way knowledge is shared. Indeed, sharing knowledge is not in itself anything new. What is, however, is the sharing of virtual trust. This informal contractual mechanism is the driving force behind the development of network cooperation. It is also the key to the development of collective intelligence. This is why a multitude of collaborative tools and automated filters are being developed to streamline decisions and choices on the Web. These agents filter the information available in the global brain to reveal neural groups, i.e. individuals sharing the same opinions or interests. This is how online subcultures are created, of which communities and blogs are only the most visible showcase.

The fourth characteristic I identified in collective intelligence is the implementation of a "project", a goal to be reached, a result to be achieved. This characteristic is the most problematic. It raises the question of what, if anything, the global brain is trying to achieve. As a project, what we see today is the profusion of technologies designed to increase intelligence. But whose intelligence are we talking about, that of humans or that of the superorganism? Is it the intelligence of machines, increasingly destined to hybridize with human intelligence in the global brain? What is the project behind this immense technological deployment? In the words of Günther Anders, the race for intelligence in machines is "unquenchable". The exponential growth in computing power predicted by Moore's Law is confirmed every day. Memory capacity has increased by leaps and bounds, as has miniaturization. Quantum computers have passed the prototype stage, and so-called biological or DNA computers should be operational within the next ten years. We are in the ascendant part of an extremely rapid development curve that affects not just computers, but a considerable number of objects that will become increasingly intelligent and interconnected. The law of development for these machines is to break down the boundary between human and artificial intelligence. Ray Kurzweil, one of the world's leading authorities on the subject, now prefers to speak of "augmented intelligence"[287] to underline the inevitable fusion between man and machine. Artificial Intelligence is based on modeling living organisms to reproduce their functions[288]. This requires considerable computing power, which is possible today and will be even more so tomorrow. Hans Moravec, one of the fathers of intelligent robotics, believes that we are in the midst of an evolutionary mutation[289]. A metatransition brought about by the exponential explosion in computing power at the service of hyperinformational objects. Moravec speaks of a "singularity", i.e. a zero point from which an entirely new universe will emerge. Where *Homo sapiens 2.0* will appear.

The symbiosis that is taking place between human organisms and artificial entities is transforming utopias or the beginnings of collective intelligence, into the very concrete and immediate prospects of augmented intelligence. This opens up a radically new field in human history. The hyperinformational force they have unleashed and made their daily life now enters the microworlds of biology and matter. A phenomenon of immeasurable scope is taking place: intelligence is penetrating fields that were previously inert or off-limits, producing a new form of hybridization in which man is at once the producer, the subject and the object. Every day, the tintamarresque news informs us of a new technological breakthrough in a hitherto forbidden territory: the gene itself. Genetic engineering, with its restriction enzymes, ligases and transfer vectors, has discovered the language of molecular programming, transforming biology into the "science of biological

---

287. KURZWEIL (Ray), *The Age of Spiritual Machines*, Penguin Books, 1999.
288. Examples of successful synthesis of simple DNA, such as that of the poliomyelitis virus, already show the way: scanning and digitizing living matter to recreate artificial equivalents capable of interfacing with that same living matter.
289. MORAVEC (Hans), *Robot*, Oxford University Press, 1999.

information processing[290]". The workings of the microworlds of biology became the models for the new alchemists of matter. By taking a closer look at the structure of molecular membranes[291], proteins, DNA itself, the micromotors at the heart of cells, microtubules and flagella, and drawing inspiration from them, engineers are creating "intelligent materials", implantable biotechnology chips, and molecular machines capable of machining nanometric materials. They now know how to direct human cells, especially nerve cells, so that they repair themselves in the event of injury, and how to implant miniaturized reservoirs of medicinal substances delivered when and where they are needed in the human organism. The techniques of the 21st century possess the secret of combining the living and the artificial. They know how to place, at the heart of our most ordinary machines, molecular microcomponents, hybrids made of silicon and living cells, neurochips that cultivate living neurons in their silicon support, biotransistors with a computing capacity far beyond their simply electronic predecessors, which can be controlled and piloted remotely. They can directly link the computer to the living world by installing bioelectronic interfaces between man and machine, producing links of intelligence in which both are hybridized. These "feats" are not futuristic fantasies; they are the results of work *currently being* carried out all over the planet by a host of researchers whose genius is being relentlessly challenged by economic competition and memetic selection. This research, designed to infuse hyperinformation into every aspect of matter and life, is revealing more and more of its impact on our daily lives, now and in the very near future.

Today's Internet landscape is but a pale prefiguration of the global brain that is taking shape thanks to the convergence of mastery of wire-

---

290. ROSNAY (Joël de), "De la biologie moléculaire à la biotique : l'essor des bio-, info- et nanotechnologies", in *Cellular and Molecular Biology*, n° 47, 2001, p. 7-16.
291. Thanks in particular to "tunneling microscopes".

less communication networks, geolocation and the miniaturization of augmented intelligence enabled by info-, bio- and nanotechnologies. At present, hyperinformation circulates via telecommunications networks, but several laboratories are working on a project to break free from these networks and connect humans directly to each other and to their machines. We can now use body networks that rely on the conductivity of the skin to transmit a signal between various pieces of equipment worn by an individual[292]. You can already exchange your electronic business card with a simple handshake[293]. Without going to these extremes, wireless networks on a local or global scale are becoming more and more diversified and sophisticated, enabling images, sounds, texts and all the data recorded by billions of sensors on the planet to be transited and exchanged everywhere. Among these sensors, the population of RFID chips is growing exponentially, already far outnumbering humans. These chips, whether active or passive, are set to be integrated into every aspect of our lives: in our bodies, in the form of identification or medical control implants[294], but also in all the objects of our daily lives: from the pack of washing powder bought at the supermarket to the refrigerator installed in your

---

292. These intelligent garments herald the arrival of "*wearable* computers".

293. In 2003, Japanese researchers at NTT DoCoMo created a network using the human body as infrastructure. The ElectAura-Net network is wireless, and does not use radio waves, infrared light or microwaves to transmit information: it uses a combination of the electric field emanating from the human body and sensors to capture it. This network solution, currently confined to the home (floors and ceilings need to be fitted with suitable sensors), enables data rates of the order of 10 Mb/s (see internetactu.net/index.php ?p=4065).

294. Several very concrete projects are now based on the implantation of subcutaneous chips in animals, and even in humans. A Spanish nightclub is already offering its customers a subcutaneous chip to facilitate entry and payment for drinks. The US *Food and Drug Administration* has given the *Verichip* company the go-ahead to implant an RFID identification chip under the skin of patients. And British pioneer Kevin Warwick is looking forward to 2015, when chips will be implanted in the brain, enabling us to communicate by thought, including remotely via the Internet. Cf. CORNU (Jean-Michel) & KAPLAN (Daniel), *ProspecTic* 2010, FING, Irepp, 2005.

kitchen. These "intelligent objects" are an integral part of the global brain, transmitting multiple types of information and localizing the objects they inhabit. They are able to sense and act on their environment, whether it's a physical space, a machine or a body. They are linked together in autonomous networks[295], forming the immaterial synapses of the global superorganism. What's more, their miniaturization enables them to be transformed into microscopic *smart* dust[296].

Technological convergence also concerns *intelligent agents*, autonomous computer programs capable of making decisions without external intervention, choosing their own actions to achieve a set objective. Coupled with the multiple sensors constituted by the population of intelligent objects, these agents become the intelligence particles of the global brain. They continue their virtual existence, and can communicate with other agents, act in the network and move around within it. Their cooperation, implemented in the form of "multi-agent systems", multiplies their working power, their adaptability to their environment and their ability to solve increasingly complex tasks. Such systems, hybrids of hardware and digital technology, are evolutionary and cooperative; they are ultimately capable of autonomously constructing material bodies, arranging and organizing themselves into societies that are increasingly independent of man. Psychologist and philosopher Jean-Michel Truong, a specialist in artificial intelligence, calls them *successors*: "I call *successor* that new form of life likely to take over from man as the habitat of consciousness[297]". They are the links destined to succeed us in Darwinian evolution. The progress of

---

295. Work is underway in the USA and Europe to develop autonomous networks capable of configuring, optimizing and protecting themselves by 2020.

296. The first products, delivered in 2004, are designed to be scattered by the thousands in forests to trigger an immediate alert in the event of fire. The slightest spark triggers a message that is automatically transmitted from dust to dust, in the same way as the stigmergy of ants, which I've already mentioned.

297. Cf. TRUONG (Jean-Michel), *Totally inhuman*, Seuil, 2001.

220

intelligent agents and robotics raises questions that cannot be put off into the distant future, because their presence is immediate. The uses of domestic, professional, civil and military robots are multiplying unchecked. Their miniaturization, biomimicry, intelligence and ability to cooperate all point to a bright future. Whether connected to humans or autonomous, their development is unstoppable. As is the total immersion of humans in their own projections. Constantly connected, identified, controlled and "traced", *Homo sapiens 2.0* will find it increasingly difficult to distinguish the real from the virtual. Evolving in an environment whose every nook and cranny will be intelligent, from the electronic wall to the tactile floor, the atoms of his body itself will integrate the bits of a new augmented intelligence. He'll be able to feel and communicate with the fullness of his five senses: touch, taste, smell, sight and hearing. His emotions will be shared by the machines, understood, anticipated or developed, connected to the distance, to others, by the hyperinformational current.

An immense super-network will cover the Earth like a communications skin. "Watch the intelligent crowds emerge," exclaims Howard Rheingold[298]. Equipped with chips that communicate with each other, computers that know where they are, wearable technologies like jewels, connected to everyone and everything, drunk with knowledge available but forever unfulfilled, these new crowds arrive with their processions of hopes and utopias. Is the goal of their long march the predicted mega-merger or the promised land of a better world? The metatransition to *Homo sapiens 2.0* holds the potential for unprecedented transformations. The immense convergence of nanotechnologies, biotechnologies, information technologies and cognitive sciences is opening up unprecedented horizons. It undoubtedly raises

---

298. RHEINGOLD (Howard), *Foules intelligentes, la révolution qui commence*, M2 Éditions, 2005.

hopes, but also risks and questions of a truly metaphysical nature. Hopes that we will be able to use augmented collective intelligence to find better solutions to the challenges we face in terms of climate, ageing populations, access to healthcare, pollution and energy. Risks, too, in the face of the conceptual, technical, economic, societal and even philosophical uncertainties that this transformation is bound to produce. *Homo sapiens, once* again, overwhelmed by its power, perhaps for the last time. Or *Homo sapiens 2.0*, more intelligent, more cooperative, freer to live and feel, having reached the culminating point, the Teilhardian *Omega*, of its evolution.

Interlude XII

Letters to future generations

At the turn of the millennium, Unesco asked twenty-two authors of all nationalities to send a message to future generations[299]. Here are a few extracts:

> *"Don't forget the poetry! Without poetry, the world will be one-eyed and lame. Without poetry, mankind will lose a little more of its soul every day. Without poetry, the Earth will be flat, the sea will lose its blue and foam, the sky will be indifferent and children will no longer clamor for bedtime stories."*

> Tahar BEN JELLOUN, writer (Morocco)

> *"Imagine, then, that each of us, gifted with multiple intelligences, gave one thousandth of our true wealth to every passer-by we met on the first street corner or on the other side of the world. We'll have the horizon at our feet, the most beautiful foundation of the*

---

299. *Lettres aux générations futures*, unpublished texts by twenty-two authors compiled by Frederico MAYOR and Roger-Pol DROIT, UNESCO Publishing Paris, 1999.

habitable place. But that's just a dream, isn't it? You can safely devote time to this dream."

Tanella BONI, philosopher (Ivory Coast)

"We now know that we are dots in an immense universe, much larger than we thought only a hundred years ago. On Earth, we have 3.5 billion years of accumulated genetic information. Each individual is therefore not a creation, but comes from biological structures sketched out 3 and a half billion years ago, when the first memory molecules were formed. We need to be aware that each individual is a link in an extremely long chain. This is both humbling and great, because we are aware of all that has gone before us.

Luc MONTAGNIER, biologist (France)

"Choose life! These three words sum up what I'd like to say to you, the inheritors of this planet. In the course of my life, I've seen the world radically transformed, thanks to extraordinary technological advances. I've been able to do things my grandparents wouldn't have dared dream of. New horizons are opening up every day. Yet deep down inside, we humans haven't changed much. We are still guided by a hunger that too often turns into insatiable greed, by a passion that too often turns to uncontrollable violence. Choose life!"

David M. NEUHAUS s.j., theologian (Israel)

"The future is not given. The great French historian Bernard Braudel once wrote: "Events are dust." Is this true? But what is an event? The analogy with "bifurcations" (studied above

all in non-equilibrium physics) immediately springs to mind. These bifurcations appear at singular points where the trajectory followed by a system subdivides into "branches". All branches are possible, but only one will be realized. A bifurcation doesn't usually occur on its own; rather, a succession of bifurcations appears. This leads to a historical, narrative aspect, even in the basic sciences. It's the "end of certainties", the title of my latest book. The world is a construction, a construction in which we can all participate."

Ilya PRIGOGINE, Nobel Prize in Chemistry (Belgium)

"Let's make sure there are still people around to celebrate the beginning of the 21st century. That's the responsibility of all of us.

Hubert REEVES, astrophysicist (Canada)

"Whether it's music, art, painting, sculpture, the wonders of nature, we risk forgetting them in front of a computer screen, never leaving home. Sooner or later, we won't be able to see the sky. We won't even pay attention to the trees along the road that takes us from home to work. Don't get me wrong, I'm afraid we'll be hypnotized by screens, by the flood of data we don't necessarily need. It seems to me that we're more enriched by taking part in culture, in the history of our country, in architecture, painting or music. Then you reach a whole new sphere: the emotional sphere of your own perception of life, where love, children and family are born. It's not just a question of reproduction - excuse the vulgarity of the expression - but of human relations, of love for others, and it takes time.

Mstislav ROSTROPOVITCH, musician (Russian Federation)

"Faust's double metamorphosis - I mean rejuvenation and trans-figuration - is perhaps also the destiny of future generations.

Darius SHAYEGAN, philosopher (Islamic Republic of Iran)

"The life you're living is not lacking anything, but it doesn't have anything new that's really important and hitherto unknown. You're in the place where man has always been, and you're facing the same challenge as we or our forebears. You are confronted with the same fatal strangeness of the here and now. The setting and staging change, but the old drama continues.
Your true instruments will never be the latest technology, but love and hate, compassion and cruelty, lies and truth. The oldest things, the ones that never fail and never slip away. Prepare to become unique, original and fragile beings? as we all have been, and as every woman and man will continue to be. Don't believe the prophets who announce the end of times and the arrival of a new era, or another Messiah. Don't believe them, but above all don't have the weakness to believe that you need them or that it's useful to get what they promise."

Fernando SAVATER, philosopher (Spain)

13. Homo sapiens 2.0

In 1950, Teilhard de Chardin wrote: "The truly explosive development of technology and research; the theoretical and practical seizure of the secrets and springs of cosmic energy in all its degrees and forms; and, correlatively, the rapid rise in what we have called the psychic temperature of the Earth... If we know how to look beyond the surface chaos, is this not the spectacle we are witnessing? A human tide that lifts us irresistibly, with all the force of a contracting star; a tide that is not flat, as we might have thought, but in full ascension crisis: the relentless rise, on our horizon, of a veritable 'ultra-human'[300]." This groundswell, which is sweeping through human societies in general and every human being in particular, is caused by the onslaught of hyperinformation. Its froth is made up of half-inert, half-intelligent objects that swarm together to form entities, organisms and humans of a new species, connected together in a gigantic *chimera*, an assemblage of bits and matter. This new form of life doesn't originate in the iridescent Proterozoic ponds I described at the start of this book, but on our current good old planet, here and now.

Rest assured, we're not in a situation often depicted in science fiction literature with its mutants, cyborgs and other more or less friendly

---

300. TEILHARD DE CHARDIN (Pierre), "Sur l'existence probable, en avant de nous d'un *ultra-humain*" (1950), in *L'Avenir de l'homme*, Seuil, 1959.

creatures. I can assure you that green antennae will not be growing from the top of your skull for the foreseeable future.

The metatransition to *Homo sapiens 2.0* I'm talking about is the fruit of the natural history of hyperinformation; it's a pure product of Darwinian evolution, combining man and his projections. It is no more finalized or controlled than any other evolutionary phenomenon. Remember "The Blind Watchmaker". Admittedly, this development is taking place at an accelerated pace, which makes it unprecedented in the entire history of the evolution of species. But the results of the evolutionary thrust are the same as elsewhere, and are reflected as always in physical and ecological changes.

Man changes in his body. More precisely, his body is being supplemented, enhanced and, to some extent, augmented. Our bodies are *supplemented by* objects that externalize functions in the form of interconnected prostheses. Tomorrow, our cell phones and personal computers will certainly become implantable chips with multiple functionalities. But already, many technological tools are prostheses we can't imagine doing without. Our bodies are *enhanced* by biomedical techniques. In particular, they are responsible for increasing our lifespan. Bio- and nanotechnologies will further improve our physical performance through repairs and implants, of which artificial corneas and pacemakers are only the most rudimentary foretaste. The *augmented* human being is the one to whom neurotechnologies will implant interfaces for direct connection to the great global brain. He will also be the one who selects himself, reproducing by cloning the best of what he thinks he is. These are the ethical barriers and limits beyond which we enter Aldous Huxley's *Brave New World*.

Man is changing his ecology, i.e. his memetic, cultural and societal niche. Hyperinformation technologies bring *Homo sapiens 2.0* into contact with an ever-expanding and ever-more complex universe of knowledge. What's more, the human being is engaged in a process in which he is no longer a mere spectator or consumer of knowledge; he

228

is also a producer, constantly plugged into the super-organism, transferring his memes, inventing them, exchanging them and enriching them with others. This permanent cross-fertilization of ideas, values and cultures on a global scale is disrupting the ecological coherence of human societies. Engaged in a Darwinian evolution, memes will find themselves in head-on conflict with certain values that have held people together for centuries. Some will give up, after a few rearguard actions; others, on the contrary, will resist, taking up the weapons of fanaticism. The mutations produced by the evolution towards *Homo sapiens 2.0* will arouse against them the ardent defenders of lost values. But new values will undoubtedly emerge, perhaps even a new civilization.

Will *Homo sapiens 2.0* have the moral values on which humanism was founded? It will have to if it is to hold its own against *Homo demens*, ever present with its destructive impulses and even more devastating means. The boundary between them is thinner than ever, but also more fragile. Nietzsche rightly thought that "the greatness of Man is that he is a bridge and not an end"; what we can love about him "is that he is *transition* and *perdition*[301]." The ideals of cooperation, altruism and humanism will be essential components of the immune system that the superorganism will have to secrete to combat the invasion of destructive pathogenic cells. Elitism, exclusion, compartmentalization, the surveillance and control society: these are just some of the many enemies that threaten *Homo sapiens 2.0*, and whose first troops are already taking up battle positions. *Homo sapiens 2.0* will have to fight fiercely to impose itself. The future of humanity and the survival of the biosphere will be insufficient arguments to win the battle. He can call on the reserve army of non-human entities endowed with bionic intelligence that he himself has created, but that won't be enough. For his main enemy will be the very thing he has

---

301. NIETZSCHE (Friedrich), *Thus Spoke Zarathustra*, I, 3-4.

created. His future lies in his hands; it will be what he makes of it, for he is now capable of producing the kind of human he wants to become. But he doesn't know it. And what's more, he has no power to control the river of evolution whose current he himself has fed. All his choices, all his decisions, every single one of his actions will be subject to the law of selection, whether genetic or memetic. His will, his free will, the principles to which he is so intimately attached, will be mere *emergences*. His decisions will be the result of involuntary processes beyond his human scale. His actions will be diluted in the flow of unexpected phenomena, depriving them of any voluntaristic significance. This is, by nature, the nature of man's projections: they are beyond him. Today, more than ever, the slightest action has an unpredictable deadly or fruitful impact. Man has crossed the threshold of excessive power. The coming climatic cataclysm is just one of many visible manifestations of this.

And yet, you may object, science is progressing, knowledge is expanding in unprecedented proportions, our ability to grasp reality seems to be growing exponentially, and the mesh of human and artificial intelligence is becoming ever finer and more intertwined. All true. But where is it all heading? We're not aware of it, because *we can't* have a higher consciousness, i.e. a consciousness outside the superorganism we've created. A self-referential system like ours has no *reflexive* capacity. It cannot look at itself from the outside and measure the impact of its actions. The "reflection" I'm talking about here is not what Aristotle, for example, considered the "thinking" part of the soul. Nor is it the structure of a transcendental subject as Kant understood it; nor is it Fichte's "self-consciousness". It corresponds to that broadening of a system's perspective, described by Niklas Luhmann, which would consist in the awareness of its identity not only in relation to itself, but in relation to others and to its future identity. A super-organism, however sophisticated, is not capable of this virtue, as it is by definition closed in on itself. The only way this reflexive attitude can emerge is from outside. But which one? It's hard to answer. Philosopher Jean-Pierre Dupuy tells us that we should certainly accept our destiny, which relieves us of the burden of autonomy[302]. On the contrary, I believe that the battle is not lost, and that the systems of knowledge and intelligence that are being deployed more and more each day could awaken our consciousness, and pull us away from the gravitational pull of a super-organism hurtling along. The reach of our minds can be broadened and accelerated by hyperinformation. It can lift our self-centred *ego out* of its pettiness, giving it an open vision and a global dimension. A consciousness on the scale of the human species and the planet. Hyperinformation technologies are our projection, but also our extension. The resulting connected intelligence endows us with performative powers: our thoughts and the way we express them now possess an increased capacity to transform reality. But we have to want it, because that requires courage and certainly an immense ethic of responsibility[303], an ethic capable of simply saying no, when *bonum humanum*, the human good, is threatened.

To conclude, I'd like to leave you to ponder on these words by Sartre, which crystallize the tragic dilemma of *Homo sapiens 2.0*: "Those who hide their total freedom from themselves, by a spirit of seriousness or by deterministic excuses, I will call cowards; those who try to show that their existence was necessary, when it is the very contingency of man's appearance on earth, I will call bastards[304]."

---

302. Cf. Dupuis (Jean-Pierre), *Pour un catastrophisme éclairé*, Seuil, 2002.
303. Cf. Jonas (Hans), *Pour une éthique du futur*, Payot, 1998.
304. Sartre (Jean-Paul), *L'existentialisme est un humanisme*, Nagel, 1946.

Postscript

"What kind of chimera is man? What a novelty, what a monster, what chaos, what a subject of contradiction, what a prodigy!"

Pascal, *Pensées*, 1680.

Bibliography

Allègre (Claude), *Introduction à une Histoire naturelle*, Fayard, 1992.

Anders (Günther), *L'Obsolescence de l'homme*, Éditions de l'encyclopédie des nuisances & Éditions Ivrea, 2002.

—, *Nous, fils d'Eichmann*, Payot & Rivages, 2003.

Aristotle, *The Poetics*, trans. Roselyne Dupont-Roc and Jean Lallot, Seuil, 1980.

Arnould (Jacques), *Dieu versus Darwin. Les créationnistes vont-ils triompher de la science*, Albin Michel, 2007.

Arthus-Bertrand (Yann), *La Terre vue du ciel*, Éditions La Martinière, 1999.

Asch (Salomon), *Groups, Leadership and Men*, Pittsburgh, Carnegie Press, 1951.

Aunger (Robert), *The Electric Meme. A New Theory of How we Think*, Cambridge, The Free Press, 2002.

Axelrod (Robert), *Comment réussir dans un monde d'égoïstes*, Odile Jacob, 1996.

Ayache (Gérard), *La Grande Confusion*, France Europe Éditions, 2006.

Barkow (Jerome H.), Cosmides (Leda) & Tooby (John), *The Adapted Mind: Evolutionary Psychology and the Generation of Culture*, Oxford University Press, 1992.

Basalla (Georges), *The Evolution of Technology*, Cambridge University Press, 1989.

Bataille (Georges), *Lascaux ou la Naissance de l'art*, Geneva, Albert Skira, 1980.

—, *Les Larmes d'Éros*, Pauvert, 2001.

Bateson (Gregory), *Vers une écologie de l'esprit, Seuil, 1991.*

Ben-Jacob (Eshel), "Bacterial Self-Organization: Co-Enhancement of Complexication and Adaptability in a Dynamic Environment", in *Philosophical Transactions of the Royal Society*, vol. 361, no. 1807, June 15, 2003.

— & Levine (Herbert), "The Artistry of Nature", in *Nature*, n° 409, 2001.

Bergson (Henri), *Les Deux Sources de la morale et de la religion*, PUF, 1932.

—, *Essai sur les données immédiates de la conscience (1889)*, PUF, 2003.

Berners-Lee (Tim), *Weaving the Web: The Original Design and Ultimate Destiny of the World Wide Web by Its Inventor*, Harper Business, 2000.

Blackmore (Susan), *The Evolution of Meme Machines*, paper presented at the International Congress of Ontopsychology and Memetics, Milan, May 18-21, 2002.

—, *La Théorie des mèmes. Why we imitate each other*, Max Milo, 2006.

Bloom (Howard), *The Lucifer Principle, tome I*, Le Jardin des livres, 2001.

—, *Lucifer Principle. Le cerveau global*, Le Jardin des livres, 2003.

Bonabeau (Eric) & Theraulaz (Guy), "Swarm Smarts", in *Scientific American*, n° 282, p. 72-79, 2000.

Bourdieu (Pierre) & Passeron (Jean-Claude), *La Reproduction*, Éditions de Minuit, 1970.

Boyer (Pascal), *Et l'homme créa les dieux*, Robert Laffont, 2001.

Brack (André) & Raulin (François), *L'Évolution chimique et les origines de la vie*, Dunod, 1997.

Brun (Jean), *Les Masques du désir*, Buchet Chastel, 1994.

Buisseret (Pierre), *Pas si bêtes ! Mille cerveaux, mille mondes*, Nathan, Coll. du Muséum national d'histoire naturelle, 1999.

Buisseret (Pierre), "Évolution du cerveau et intelligence", in *L'intelligence*, ed. Jacques Lautrey and Jean-François Richard, Lavoisier, 2005.

Canclini (Nestor Garcia), *Culturas hibridas*, Ediciones Paidos Iberica, 2001.

Cavalli-Sforza (Luca), *Gènes, peuples & langues*, Odile Jacob, 1996.

Certeau (Michel de), *L'Invention du quotidien, I. Arts de faire*, Gallimard, 1990.

Chaline (Jean), *What's new since Darwin? La théorie de l'évolution dans tous ses états*, Ellipses, 2006.

Chamak (Brigitte), "Sciences cognitives et modèles de pensée", in *Sens public*, September 2004.

Changeux (Jean-Pierre), *L'Homme neuronal*, Fayard, 1983.

—, *L'Homme de vérité*, Odile Jacob, 2004.

Charpak (Georges) & Omnès (Roland), *Soyez savants, devenez prophètes*, Odile Jacob, 2004.

Chomsky (Noam), *Language and Thought*, Payot, 1990.

Coppens (Yves), *Pré-ambules : les premiers pas de l'homme*, Odile Jacob, 2001.

Cornu (Jean-Michel) & Kaplan (Daniel), *ProspecTic* 2010, FING, Irepp, 2005.

Crick (Francis), *A Life to Discover. From the double helix to memory, Odile Jacob, 1989.*

Damasio (Antonio), *L'erreur de Descartes: la raison des émotions*, Odile Jacob, 1995.

—, *Le Sentiment même de soi, Odile Jacob*, 1999.

Dantec (Maurice G.), *Millenium Machines*, 1998 (unedited text, available online at mauricedantec.com).

Darwin (Charles), *The Origin of Species by Means of Natural Selection (1859)*, La Découverte, 1989.

Dawkins (Richard), *The Selfish Gene*, Armand Colin, 1990.

—, *Qu'est-ce que l'évolution? Le fleuve de la vie*, Hachette Littératures, 1997.

—, *L'Horloger aveugle (1986)*, Robert Laffont, 1999.

Deacon (Terence W.), *The Symbolic Species. The Co-Evolution of Language and the Brain*, New York, W. W. Norton & Cie, 1997.

Deleuze (Gilles) & Guattari (Félix), *Mille Plateaux (Capitalisme et schizophrénie, tome II)*, Éditions de Minuit, 1980.

Dennett (Daniel), *Consciousness Explained*, Odile Jacob, 1993.

—, *Darwin est-il dangereux*, Odile Jacob, 2000.

Dick (Philip K.), "Ce que disent les morts", short story from *Minority Report*, Gallimard, 2006.

Dobzhansky (Theodosius), *Biology of Ultimate Concern*, New York American Library, 1967.

Dupuy (Jean-Pierre), *Aux origines des sciences cognitives*, La Découverte, 1999.

—, *Pour un catastrophisme éclairé*, Seuil, 2002.

Durkheim (Émile), *Formes élémentaires de la vie religieuse (1912)*, PUF, 1998.

Eccles (John C.), *Evolution of the Brain and the Creation of Consciousness*, Flammarion, 1994.

Eco (Umberto), *Sémiotique et philosophie du langage*, PUF, 1992.

Edelman (Gerald D.M.) & Tononi (Giulio), *How matter becomes consciousness*, Odile Jacob, 2001.

Edelman (Gerald D.M.), *Vaster than the Sky. A new general theory of the brain*, Odile Jacob, 2004.

—, *Second Nature. Brain, Science and Human Knowledge*, Yale University Press, 2007.

Eliade (Mircea), *La Nostalgie des origines*, Gallimard, 1971.

Elias (Norbert), *The Dynamics of the West*, Calmann-Lévy, 1994.

ELLUL (Jacques), *Le Bluff technologique*, Hachette, 1988.

—, *La Technique ou l'Enjeu du siècle*, Economica, [2nd] ed., 1999.

ESPAGNAT (Bernard d'), *À la recherche du réel*, Gauthier-Villars, 1979.

FINKIELKRAUT (Alain), *L'Humanité perdue. Essai sur le XXe siècle*, Seuil, 1996.

FISHER (Helen E.), *The Strategy of Sex*, Calmann-Lévy, 1982.

FODOR (Jerry A.), *The Modularity of the Mind*, Éditions de Minuit, 1986.

FOERSTER (Heinz von), *Principles of Self Organisation*, New York, Pergamon, 1962.

FREEMAN (Walter J.), *How Brains Make up Their Minds*, Columbia University Press, 2001.

FREUD (Sigmund), *Totem and Taboo (1913)*, Payot, 1947.

FRISCH (Karl von), *Vie et mœurs des abeilles*, Albin Michel, 1984.

GAINES (Brian R.), "The Collective Stance in Modeling Expertise in Individuals and Organizations", in *International Journal of expert Systems*, n° 71, pp. 22-51, 1994.

GARDNER (Howard), *History of the Cognitive Revolution. The new science of the mind*, Payot, 1993.

GAUCHET (Marcel), *Le Désenchantement du monde*, Gallimard, 1985.

GIRARD (René), *Mensonge romantique et vérité romanesque*, Hachette, 1999.

—, *Les Origines de la culture*, Desclée de Brouwer, 2004.

GOFFMAN (Erving), *Études sur la condition sociale des malades mentaux*, Éditions de Minuit, 1968.

GOULD (Stephen Jay), *La vie est belle*, Seuil, 1991.

—, *La Structure de la théorie de l'évolution*, Gallimard, 2006.

GRAMSCI (Antonio), *Cahiers de prison*, Gallimard, 1983.

HALL (Edward T.), *Beyond Culture*, Seuil, 1979.

HAMEROFF (Stuart R.), *Ultimate Computing: Biomolecular Consciousness and Nanotechnology*, Elsevier Science Ltd, 1987.

HAYEK (Friedrich August von), *The Road to Serfdom*, PUF, 1993.

Hebb (Donald O.), *The Organization of Behavior: A Neuropsychological Theory*, New York, Wiley, 1949.

Heylinghen (Francis) & Bollen (Johan), "The World Wide Web as a Super Brain: from Metaphor to Model", in *Cybernetics and systems*, Austrian Society for Cybernetics, 1996.

Heylinghen (Francis), "Conception of a Global Brain: an historical review", in *Technical Forecasting and Social Change*, 2004.

Hobbes (Thomas), *Leviathan (1651)*, Gallimard, 2000.

Hottois (Gilbert), *Le Signe et la Technique*, Aubier, 1984.

Humphrey (Nicholas), *The Inner Eye: Social Intelligence in Evolution*, Oxford University Press, 2002.

Huxley (Aldous), *Brave New World (1932)*, Pocket, 2002.

Jacob (François), *La Logique du vivant*, Gallimard, 1970.

Janis (Irving), *Groupthink. Psychological Studies of Policies Decisions and Fiascoes*, Boston, Houghton Mifflin Company, 1982.

Jonas (Hans), *Pour une éthique du futur*, Payot, 1998.

—, *Évolution et liberté*, Payot & Rivages, 2000.

Jouxtel (Pascal), *Comment les systèmes pondent. Introduction à la mémétique*, Vuibert, 2005.

Keller (Laurent) & Gordon (Élisabeth), *La Vie des fourmis*, Odile Jacob, 2006.

Kerckhove (Derrick de), *L'Intelligence des réseaux*, Odile Jacob, 2000.

Kurzweil (Ray), *The Age of Spiritual Machines*, Penguin Books, 1999.

Laïdi (Zaki), *Le Sacre du présent*, Flammarion, 2000.

Laplanche (Jean) & Pontalis (Jean-Bertrand), *Vocabulaire de la psychanalyse*, PUF, 1998.

Le Bon (Gustave), *Psychologie des foules*, PUF, 1947.

Leroi-Gourhan (André), *Milieu et techniques*, Albin Michel, 1945.

Le Roy (Édouard), *Les Origines humaines et l'évolution de l'intelligence*, Boivin et Cie, 1931.

Lévi-Strauss (Claude), *Anthropologie structurale (1958)*, Plon, 1996.

Lévy (Pierre), *Les Technologies de l'intelligence*, La Découverte, 1990.

—, *L'Intelligence collective*, La Découverte, 1997.

Lévy-Bruhl (Lucien), *L'Âme primitive (1927)*, PUF, 1963.

—, *Le Surnaturel et la nature dans la mentalité primitive (1931)*, PUF, 1963.

Lewis (Roy), *Pourquoi j'ai mangé mon père*, Actes Sud, 1990.

Lovelock (James E.), *The Earth is a Living Being. The Gaia Hypothesis*, Éditions du Rocher, 1990.

Luhmann (Niklas), *Politique et complexité*, Cerf, 1999.

—, *La Confiance, un mécanisme de réduction de la complexité sociale*, Economica, 2006.

Lynch (Aaron), *Thought Contagion: How Belief Spreads through Society*, New York, Basic Books, 1996.

—, "An Introduction to Evolutionary Epidemiology of Ideas", in *The Biological Physicist*, vol. 3, no. 2, 2003, pp. 7-13.

Mac Orlan (Pierre), *Petit Manuel du parfait aventurier (1920)*, Mercure de France, 1998.

Margenau (Henry), *Miracle of Existence*, Ox Bow Pr. 1984.

Margulis (Lynn), *Symbiosis in Cell Evolution. Life and Its Environment on the Early Earth*, New York, Freeman, 1981.

— & Sagan (Dorion), *L'Univers bactériel: les nouveaux rapports de l'homme et de la nature*, Albin Michel, 1989.

— & Dolan (Michael F.), *Early Life: Evolution on the Precambrian Earth*, Jones & Bartlett Publishers, Sudbury - Massachusetts, 2001.

Marshack (Alexander), *Hierarchical Evolution of the Human Capacity: The Paleolithic Evidence*, New York, American Museum of Natural History, 1985.

Maturana (Humberto) & Varela (Francisco), *Autopoiesis and Cognition: The Realization of the Living*, Springer, 1979.

Mauss (Marcel), "Essai sur le don", in *L'Année sociologique*, seconde série, 1923-1924.

Millet (Jean-Philippe), *L'Absolu technique: Heidegger et la question de la technique*, Kimé, 2000.

Monod (Jacques), *Le Hasard et la Nécessité*, Seuil, 1970.

Morand (Paul), *Rien que la Terre (1925)*, Grasset, 2000.

Moravec (Hans), *Mind Children: The Future of Robot and Human Intelligence*, Harvard University Press, 1990.

—, *Robot*, Oxford University Press, 1999.

Morel (Christian), *Les Décisions absurdes. Sociologie des erreurs radices et persistantes*, Gallimard, 2002.

Morin (Edgar), *Le Paradigme perdu. La Nature humaine*, Seuil, 1973.

Mumford (Lewis), *Technique and Civilization*, Seuil, 1950.

Nietzsche (Friedrich), *Aurore (1881)*, Gallimard, 1989.

-*Ainsi parlait Zarathoustra (1885)*, Mercure de France, 1952.

Noubel (Jean-François), *Intelligence collective, la révolution invisible*, TheTransitioner.org, 2006.

Origgi (Gloria), "Gènes et culture", in *Dictionnaire du corps*, Michela Marzano (dir.), PUF, 2007.

Otlet (Paul), *Traité de documentation*, Éditions du Centre de lecture publique de la Communauté française de Belgique, 1989.

Paley (William), *Natural Theology, Evidences of the Existence and Attributes of the Deity (1802)*, Oxford World's Classics, 2006.

Passera (Luc), *La Véritable Histoire des fourmis*, Fayard, 2006.

Penrose (Roger), *The Shadows of the Mind. In search of a science of consciousness*, InterEditions, 1995.

Perlès (Catherine), *Préhistoire du feu*, Masson, 1977.

Piaget (Jean), *La Naissance de l'intelligence chez l'enfant (1936)*, Delachaux et Niestle, 1992.

—, *La Représentation du monde chez l'enfant (1947)*, PUF, 2003.

Pico della Mirandola (John), "De dignitate hominis" (1486), in *Œuvres philosophiques*, PUF coll. Épiméthée, 2004.

Pinker (Steven), *The Language Instinct*, Odile Jacob, 1999.

-*Comprendre la nature humaine*, Odile Jacob, 2005.

Plato, "The Republic", in *Œuvres complètes*, Gallimard, coll. La Pléiade, 1950.

Popper (Karl R.), *The Open Society and its Enemies*, Seuil, 1979.

—, *L'Univers irrésolu, plaidoyer pour l'indéterminisme*, Hermann, 1984.

— & Eccles (John C.), *The Self and Its Brain*, New York, Springer-Verlag International, 1977.

Prigogine (Ilya), *The End of Certainties*, Odile Jacob, 1996.

— & Stengers (Isabelle), *Entre le temps et l'éternité*, Fayard, 1988.

Ramachandran (Vilayanur S.), "Mirror Neurons and Imitation Learning as the Driving Force behind `the Great Leap forward' in Human Evolution", in *Edge 69*, June [1,] 2000.

Ramonet (Ignacio), *Géopolitique du chaos*, Galilée, 1997.

Rasmussen (Knud), *Across Arctic America: Narrative of the Fifth Thule Expedition (1929)*, University of Alaska, 1999.

Rheingold (Howard), *Foules intelligentes, la révolution qui commence*, M2 Éditions, 2005.

Rizzolati (Giacomo) *et al*, "Premotor Cortex and the Recognition of Motor Actions", in *Cognitive Brain Research*, n° 3, 1996, p. 131-141.

—, "Les neurones miroirs", in *Pour la Science*, n° 351, January 2007.

Rosnay (Joël de), *Le Macroscope, vers une vision globale*, Seuil, 1975.

-*L'Homme symbiotique*, Seuil, 1995.

—, "De la biologie moléculaire à la biotique : l'essor des bio-, info- et nanotechnologies", in *Cellular and Molecular Biology*, n° 47, 2001.

Rossi (Ernest), "What is life? L'évolution de l'information du flux quantique au Soi", in *Perspectives Psychologiques*, n° 26, pp. 6-22, 1992.

Ruffié (Jacques), *De la biologie à la culture*, Flammarion, 1976.

Saint-Exupéry (Antoine de), *Terre des Hommes*, Gallimard, 1939.

Sartre (Jean-Paul), *L'existentialisme est un humanisme*, Nagel, 1946.

Schrödinger (Erwin), *What is Life?* (1944), Seuil, 1993.

Serres (Michel), in *Le Point*, June 21 2007.

Shannon (Claude E.), *A Mathematical Theory of Communication*, Bell System Technical Journal, n° 27, 1948.

— & WEAVER (Warren), *The Mathematical Theory of Communication*, Chicago, Illinois University Press, 1949.

SHAPIRO (James A.), "Bacteria are small but not stupid: Cognition, Natural Genetic Engineering, and Sociobacteriology", paper published at the *Philosophical and Social Dimensions of Microbiology* conference, University of Exeter, July 2006.

SPENCER (Herbert), *The Individual versus the State*, Bibliothèque de philosophie contemporaine, 1906.

SPERBER (Dan), *The Contagion of Ideas*, Odile Jacob, 1996.

—, "An Objection to the Memetic Approach to Culture", in *Darwinizing Culture: The Status of Memetics as a Science*, Robert AUNGER (ed.), Oxford University Press, 2000.

— & WILSON (Deirdre), *Relevance: Communication and Cognition*, 2nd edition, Blackwell Publishers, 1995.

SPINOZA (Baruch), "L'Éthique, II", in *Œuvres complètes*, Gallimard, coll. La Pléiade, 1954.

STEINER (George), *La Culture contre l'homme*, Seuil, 1973.

STEWART (John), *Does life exist? Reconciling genetics and biology*, Vuibert, 2004.

STOCK (Gregory), *Metaman: The Merging of Humans and Machines into a Global Superorganism*, New York, Simon & Schuster, 1993.

STONIER (Tom), *Information and the Internal Structure of the Universe*, New York, Springer-Verlag, 1990.

TEILHARD DE CHARDIN (Pierre), *Le Phénomène humain*, Seuil, 1955.

—, *L'Avenir de l'homme*, Seuil, 1959.

THERAULAZ (Guy), "L'Intelligence collective", in *L'intelligence*, Jacques Lautrey and Jean-François Richard (eds.), Lavoisier, 2005.

THUAN (Trinh Xuan), *La Mélodie secrète*, Gallimard, 1991.

TOFFOLI (Tommaso) & MARGOLUS (Norman), *Cellular Automata Machines. A New Environment for Modeling*, Cambridge, MIT Press, 1987.

TRUONG (Jean-Michel), *Totally inhuman*, Seuil, 2001.

Turchin (Valentin), *The Phenomenon of Science, a Cybernetic Approach to Human Evolution*, New York, Colombia University Press, 1977.

Turner (Mark), *The Artful Mind: Cognitive Science and the Riddle of Human Creativity*, Oxford University Press, 2006.

Uttal (William R.), *The Psychobiology of Mind*, John Wiley & Sons Inc, 1978.

Varela (Francisco), *Autonomy and knowledge. Essai sur le vivant*, Seuil, 1989.

—, *Invitation aux sciences cognitives*, Seuil, 1996.

—, "Le cerveau n'est pas un ordinateur", interview with Hervé Kempf in *La Recherche*, n° 308, April 1998.

Virilio (Paul), *La Machine de vision*, Galilée, 1988.

—, *Cybermonde, la politique du pire*, Textuel, 1996.

Vygotsky (Lev), *Thought and Language*, Cambridge, MIT Press, 1986.

Weissberg (Jean-Louis), "Réel et virtuel", in *Multitudes*, March 1992.

Wells (Herbert G.), *World Brain*, London, Ayer Co Publications, 1938.

Wheeler (John A.), "World as System Self Synthesized by Quantum Networking", in *IBM Journal of Research and Development*, vol. 32, January 1988, pp. 4-15.

Wilson (Edward O.), *L'Humaine Nature. Essai de sociobiologie*, Stock, 1979.

—, *La Sociobiologie*, Éditions du Rocher, 1987.

Wolfram (Stephen), *A New Kind of Science*, Wolfram Media, 2002.

Table of contents

Best sellers Max Milo Editions

Hitler's banker, Jean-François Bouchard

Confessions of a forger, Éric Piedoie Le Tiec

The Koran and the flesh, Ludovic-Mohamed Zahed

Governing by fake news, Jacques Baud

Governing by chaos, Collectif

A political history of food, Paul Ariès

Mad in U.S.A.: The ravages of the "American model",
Michel Desmurget

Mondial soccer club geopolitics, Kévin Veyssière

Putin: Game master?, Jacques Braud

Treatise on the three impostors: Moses, Jesus, Muhammad,
The Spirit of Spinoza

TV Lobotomy, Michel Desmurget